Anonymus

**Catalogue of the Berlin Photographic Company**

Anonymus

**Catalogue of the Berlin Photographic Company**

ISBN/EAN: 9783742833754

Manufactured in Europe, USA, Canada, Australia, Japa

Cover: Foto ©Thomas Meinert / pixelio.de

Manufactured and distributed by brebook publishing software
(www.brebook.com)

Anonymus

**Catalogue of the Berlin Photographic Company**

# CATALOGUE

## OF THE

# BERLIN PHOTOGRAPHIC COMPANY

## FINE ART PUBLISHERS

NEW YORK

14 EAST 23D STREET

(Madison Square, South)

1896

BERLIN                    LONDON

PARIS

The Knickerbocker Press, New Rochelle, N. Y.

# CONTENTS

# PREFACE.

The results of the invention of photography appear more and more wonderful every year. Those of us who are old enough to remember its beginnings are best able to appreciate the strides towards perfection that have been made since Daguerre gave his name to a discovery from which it is to be regretted that his name was ever separated. There was something in those early daguerreotypes that appealed strongly to the imagination; they seemed in their veiled, yet clear beauty, to be softly emerging from the invisible world, the first dawnings of a creation that was yet so pleasing to the sense of wonder as to make us incurious of what the full day might bring forth. And even now, when we open those already antiquated cases, and look at their mysterious contents—having much the same charm that we find in the drawings made by the artists of the Renaissance with the silver point—we are sometimes inclined to question whether the fruits of the tree planted by Daguerre are really better worth having than these blossoms of the early spring.

But the world likes to be moving. It is never content with any past were it ever so excellent; and since the discovery of the principle that underlies the invention of Daguerre—the action of light in fixing images on sensitive surfaces—scientific men and laymen have been steadily extending the application of that principle, and bringing it nearer to perfection. So much has been already accomplished that it is difficult to see how the process of reproduction can be materially improved; nor indeed is there much left to desire in the treatment of mere black and white. The most promising field for discovery in photography to-day is in the reproduction of colors. Here, in spite of all the time, money, and skill that have been expended, we are still on the outside of the promised land. What has been done is just enough to make us eager for more.

While the reproduction by photography of works of art,—of pictures, statues, famous buildings, engravings—has vastly increased the pleasure of the world, opening up to the general public a domain that has been hitherto the almost exclusive property of a few to whom wealth and leisure gave the key; the usefulness of the invention, the practical side, has valid claims upon our respect. Students of art are indebted to it for light thrown on many a problem for whose solution comparison was necessary of work scattered through the public and private collections of Europe: collections often far apart, and in many cases difficult of access. In how many instances that might be cited, students of such problems have been led astray

iv

by dependence on copies, paintings, or engravings—the only authorities acces ole—
and in all such copies it is inevitable that the copyist should infuse sor ething
at least of himself into his work. To-day all such dependence has ceased, a d no
art-student engaged in the investigation of any serious problem would no. be
satisfied without calling in the aid of photography to illustrate his argument f
readers.

The work that has been accomplished already in providing the material for
such comparative study is enormous in quantity, and in quality so near perfection
that it may be said nothing is wanting in the case of the great etchers and engravers, and of all artists in whose work color does not play an important part.
Among the agencies that have been most active in this good work of increasing the public enjoyment, and disseminating valuable knowledge, no one has been
more conspicuous or has earned a more solid reputation than the *Berlin Photographic Company*. Its name might seem to limit its activity to the field of the great
collections of the chief German city ; but to judge so, would be to do it great
injustice. Its publications include reproductions in photography and photogravure
of the chief works, ancient and modern, that enrich the Museum of Berlin, and this
would in itself be a great service, for this museum is fast earning a place among the
foremost collections of Europe. But, beside these masterpieces of the National
Collection, other great European galleries are to be put under contribution, and their
choicest works reproduced in photography and photogravure.

Amid all this abundance of reproduction, disseminating and popularizing the
pictures of the older masters, the works of modern painters, in public or private
galleries, are by no means neglected ; and the whole history of the development of
modern art in Europe in all the chief cities is to be traced in the photographs
published by the Berlin Photographic Company. The masterpieces of men who
have carried their fame over the whole world are here put before us in a form that
makes us, in all but the one respect of color, independent of the originals. And in
many cases, even the coloring is suggested by the masterly employment of modern
discoveries that give to the blues and reds and yellows of the originals their true
value in relation to the whole color-scheme. And it may be said that in some cases
where a deficiency in the artist's color-sense has obscured the merits of his concep-
tion and arrangement, the photographs of his pictures restore him to his true place,
and explain him to those who, on seeing his works, may have found him unequal
to his reputation.

Several thousand pictures of modern and ancient artists are now represented
in this remarkable collection, far surpassing in size and quality anything that has
been reproduced anywhere else. The work of the Company has not been confined
to reproduction by photography ; it has accomplished remarkable feats in the de-
rived art of *photogravure*. In this field the Company may fairly be said to have
outstripped all its rivals, and even to challenge the finest modern engravers and
etchers in a trial of exquisite skill in workmanship. The latest publications of the
Company : the *Rembrandts of the Cassel Gallery*, the Sistine Madonna—the first
photogravure ever made from that painting—and among other modern productions,

the works of the so-called " *Secessionists* " of Munich, show the remarkable progress that has been made in this branch of the photographic art ; the very touch of the artist's brush, his peculiar manner of working—everything, in short, that distinguishes the technical method of one man from that of another, with the sole but confessedly important exception of color—is translated by this process with a perfection that seems more a work of nature than one due to the intelligence and skill of man. The reproduction by photogravure of the Cassel Rembrandts is one of the notable art-events of our time.

In these days, when so much attention is given to the art of making our homes attractive to the eye, people of taste have been quick to discover what pleasure of a solid and enduring sort is to be had from photographs of the masterpieces of painting such as are made by the Berlin Photographic Company. The large size in which many of these can be had gives them a very decorative effect when framed and hung upon the wall, and their cost is so much less than that of engravings of equal artistic value as to make them especially welcome to those whose means will not permit them to buy original paintings or water-color drawings. The money expended in fine photographs of beautiful, world-famous pictures will never be regretted, but it is a sheer waste of money to buy the works of inferior or even of second-rate artists ; and besides that nothing proves a poorer investment than such works, nothing palls sooner on the taste. The yearly annals of the auction-room, where the collections of amateurs, living and dead, are dispersed, records far more misfortunes in picture-buying than successful ventures, and many a man whose money permitted him to buy what he would, has regretted that his taste and judgment were not equal to his wealth.

But modern photography, in its different branches, offers the lover of art a wide and ever-growing collection of the noblest and most beautiful works that have been produced in past times or in our own by artists whose fame has become the property of the world ; not limited to their own country nor confined to the applause of the cultivated few. *And these splendid examples of the photographer's art are not " copies " in the ordinary sense—attempts by some artist-artisan however skilfully trained to repeat the work of an original artist—they are reproductions—reflections we may rather call them, mirror-like in their faithfulness of the work they deal with, and capable of giving the same degree of pleasure, differing only in kind, that we owe to their originals.* Secure already in the admiration of cultivated amateurs and artists, they need only to be known more widely to obtain equal favor from the general public of art-lovers.

CLARENCE COOK.

New York, July, 1894.

# CLASSIFICATION OF THIS CATALOGUE.

This Catalogue embraces several thousand original reproductions of the works of art of both old and modern masters. All classes of subjects are represented in its contents : religious, historical, allegorical, and fancy scenes, female heads and figures, hunting and sporting scenes, landscapes, etc.

The classification of the contents has been made according to practical points of view.

Of all the above pictures, with exception of reproductions *from the originals by old masters, Part III.* gives a complete list, arranged alphabetically, according to the names of the artists. It contains principally reproductions from modern masters. The limited number of classical paintings contained *in this part* are but a selection of prominent works in European galleries. These—in opposition to those given in Part V.—are not taken from the originals, but from highly finished drawings made therefrom, in which the original state of the ancient paintings, now in part damaged and darkened, has been in a large measure restored.

*Part IV.* is intended to be an appendix to Part III. For the assistance of persons not familiar with the names of artists, we have therein given a selection of popular pictures, arranged alphabetically *according to the titles*, with short explanations of the subjects. It contains also a *list of portraits* of prominent persons.

To our *Artist Proofs* and *Fac-simile Gravures in colors*, comprising a kind of *élite* edition of some of our best publications, we have given the first place in *Parts I.* and *II.*

Our reproductions taken from *the originals by old masters in European Galleries* will be found in *Part V.*, arranged alphabetically according to the artists' names, while

*Part VI.* gives a list of Art Portfolios, Albums, and also reference to Photographs from Sculptures and Views published by us. Special attention is called to our recently published portfolio, "The Rembrandts in the Cassel Gallery," and to the portfolio containing works by the Munich "Secessionists," mentioned in this part.

## COPYRIGHT.

*We publish reproductions of such modern paintings only of which we have acquired the sole right from the artist. All reproductions of the pictures mentioned in this Catalogue, not bearing in full the name of our firm (in German : Photographische Gesellschaft), are not taken from the original paintings, but are spurious imitations of our work. They must needs be of inferior quality and can by no means convey an adequate idea of the original painting.*

*We take pleasure in calling special attention to the fact that all the paintings published by us since the enactment of the International Copyright Law in the United States are protected by it, and we will accordingly enter suit against all infringements of our rights.*

# RETAIL SHOWROOMS.

Our publications are open for a leisurely inspection in any of the following showrooms :

BERLIN—Dönhofsplatz and U. D. Linden, 4a.
LONDON—133 New Bond street.
PARIS—10 Rue Vivienne.
**NEW YORK—14 East Twenty-third Street, (Madison Square, South.)**

*Orders by mail will be promptly attended to.*

## FRAMING.

We are prepared to furnish pictures framed in all styles, from neat, plain wood to the most elegant fancy frames. Suggestions on framing, estimates, etc., will be gladly furnished on application.

## ORIGINAL PAINTINGS.

In our possession are several excellent original paintings, which will be sold at extremely low prices. Among them are the following :

**C. v. Bodenhausen,** First Love.
—— Mother's Happiness.
**J. C. Herterich,** Adagio.
—— Allegro.
(Both of the above are desirable decorations for Public Halls, Concert Rooms, etc.)
**H. Hofmann,** Christ in the Garden of Gethsemane.
**H. Kaulbach,** Gretchen in Church.
**O. Lingner,** Springtime of Love.
—— Roses.
—— Violets.
**C. Müller,** The Holy Night (charcoal drawing).
(The above is a companion to the "Holy Family" in the Metropolitan Museum of Art of New York.)
**H. Outin,** Voyage de Noces.
**G. Schroedter,** Major and Minor.
—— Springtime of Roses.
—— Young Love.
**H. Sperling,** The Five Senses.
**P. Thumann,** Art Wins the Heart.

Prices of the above will be gladly furnished upon application.

viii

# I

## ARTISTS' PROOFS.

W. DENDY SADLER.

CHORUS.

"Let others sing the praise of wine;
Give me of steaming punch a bowl,
To warm the heart and cheer the soul
Fol de rol le ra la la."

I.

# ARTISTS' PROOFS.

It is well known that the first impressions from an etched or engraved copper-plate are highly appreciated by all collectors. The plate is liable to become worn out after prolonged use. Therefore the first impressions taken from it are considered the best, and their value is enhanced when they are characterized as Artists' Proofs by the original signature of the artist. To accommodate this predilection of collectors we have selected a number of our best gravure plates for an élite edition as artists' proofs. These, being the first impressions from a thoroughly finished plate, printed with the utmost care, are submitted to the painter of the original, who, as an approbation of their adequateness, signs each of them. Besides, these proofs are numbered, as a guarantee to the buyer that but a limited number of them has been issued.

How much those published by us are appreciated is best shown by the fact that a large number of them has been entirely exhausted, and that copies of the same, if accessible at all, are only to be obtained at a price much higher than the original one.

# I.—Artists' Proofs.

## Douglas Adams

WOODCOCK SHOOTING   (Size 13x21 inches.)
  200 *India Proofs*          $18 00

THE SALMON POACHER   (Size 12½x20½ inches.)
  150 *India Proofs* .          18 00

GOLDEN AUTUMN   (Size 12x20½ inches.)
  75 *India Proofs* .          18 00

## Laura Alma=Tadema

BATTLEDOOR AND SHUTTLECOCK   (Size 16x11 inches.)
  50 *Japan Proofs* .          *all sold*
  50 *India Proofs* .          *all sold*

NOTHING VENTURE, NOTHING HAVE   (Size 11x17 inches.)
  50 *Japan Proofs* .          *all sold*
  50 *India Proofs* .          *all sold*

## Lorenz Alma=Tadema

AN OLD STORY (Size 6x12 inches.)
  100 *Japan Proofs*          *all sold*
  150 *India Proofs* .          5 00

A READING FROM HOMER   (Size 17x34 inches)
  120 *India Proofs*          *all sold*

AT THE SHRINE OF VENUS   (Size 22x28 inches.)
  50 *Japan Proofs* .          *all sold*
  200 *India Proofs* .          *all sold*

LOVE IN IDLENESS   (Size 17x32⅞ inches.)
  200 *Japan Proofs*          40 00
  200 *India Proofs* .          30 00

AN EARTHLY PARADISE   (Size 15⅞x29⅞ inches.)
  250 *Japan Proofs*          60 00
  250 *India Proofs* .          48 00

SAPPHO   (Size 10⅜x19½ inches.)
  200 *India Proofs* .          15 00

PORTRAIT OF MR. PADEREWSKI   (Size 10x13 inches.)
  50 *Japan Proofs, signed by Messrs. Alma Tadema
    and Paderewski* .        18 00
  25 *India Proofs* .          *all sold*

## Lorenz Alma-Tadema

Copyright 1893, by Photographische Gesellschaft.

UNCONSCIOUS RIVALS.

UNCONSCIOUS RIVALS   (Size 14x20 inches.)

    250 *India Proofs* .                                               $30 00

IN MY STUDIO   (Size 16x12 inches.)

    100 *Japan Proofs*                                                24 00
    100 *India Proofs* .                                              18 00

## Jean Aubert

LES VOISINS DE CAMPAGNE   (Size 20½x15 inches.)

    100 *Japan Proofs*          .       .        .        20 00
    150 *India Proofs* .          .       .        .        15 00

## Eugen von Blaas

A GOURMAND   (Size 21x14¼ inches.)

    100 *Japan Proofs*                                               20 00
    150 *India Proofs* .                                              15 00

PUNCH AND JUDY   (Size 20x28½ inches.)

    100 *India Proofs* .                                              30 00

## Thomas Blinks

PARTRIDGE SHOOTING   (Size 16x20 inches.)
200 *India Proofs* .                                    $18 00

A FAIR LEAD )
GOING WELL )   (Size of each 20x14 inches)
125 *India Proofs* ,                                    18 00

A DAY WITH THE OAKLEY—Series of four paintings :
THE DRAW )
HARK AWAY |
FULL CRY  |   (Size of each 21x13 inches.)
THE FINISH )
125 *India Proofs of each*                              18 00

## W. Frank Calderon

THE ORPHANS   (Size 10x21 inches.)
300 *India Proofs* .       .       .                   18 00

## J. Cullin

RACING AT EPSOM DOWNS   (Size 17x29 inches.)
150 *India Proofs* .       .              .            15 00

## Margaret Dicksee

THE CHILD HÄNDEL   (Size 15½x21 inches.)
200 *India Proofs*       .       .               *all sold*

## A. J. Elsley

A DEAD HEAT   (Size 21x13½ inches.)
200 *India Proofs* .       .              .            18 00

GOOD BYE   (Size 21½x16½ inches.)
250 *India Proofs* .       .         .       .         18 00

## Luke Fildes

LA ZINGARELLA (Size 21x13½ inches.)
100 *Japan Proofs*       .       .    .    .    *all sold*
150 *India Proofs* .       .       .    .    .        15 00

THE VENETIANS   (Size 28½x20½ inches.)
275 *Japan Proofs*    .    .       .    .    .        40 00
175 *India Proofs* .    .    .       .    .    .      30 00

## Walther Firle

HARMONY   (Size 26x23 inches.)

    150 *India Proofs* .     .       $30 00

## Mark Fisher

NOVEMBER EVENING   (Size 20½x14½ inches.)

    50 *Japan Proofs* .       20 00
    75 *India Proofs* .       15 00

## J. W. Godward

AT THE FOUNTAIN   (Size 21x14 inches.)

    50 *Japan Proofs* .   .   .   .       24 00
    50 *India Proofs* .    .       18 00

Copyright 1893 by Photographische Gesellschaft.

MAUD GOODMAN—HUSH!

## Maud Goodman

HUSH!   (Size 14½x21 inches.)

    200 *India Proofs* .       18 00

## A. C. Gow

AFTER WATERLOO   (Size 24½x34½ inches.)

    175 *Japan Proofs*       60 00
    150 *India Proofs* .       40 00

## Keeley Halswelle

HIGHLANDS AND ISLANDS   (Size 12x21 inches.)

    50 *Japan Proofs* .       20 00
    100 *India Proofs* .       15 00

# I.—Artists' Proofs.

## L. C. Henley

SUSPENSE
CONFIDENCES } (Size 22x14 inches.)

100 *India Proofs of each* — *all sold*

## William F. Hulk

SOLITUDE  (Size 20½x11½ inches.)

100 *India Proofs* — $15 00

## G. W. Joy

TRUTH  (Size 21½x8 inches.)

50 *Japan Proofs* — 24 00
50 *India Proofs* — 18 00

## G. G. Kilburne

ALL OVER BUT THE SHOUTING  (Size 9x13 inches.)

100 *India Proofs* — 12 00

## Ridgway Knight

SHE HAS LOST HER WAY  (Size 19x15½ inches.)

100 *India Proofs* — 18 00

## B. W. Leader

THE VALLEY OF THE LLUGWY  (Size 17x28½ inches.)

200 *India Proofs* — *all sold*

EVENTIDE  (Size 16¾x19 inches.)

250 *India Proofs* — 36 00

## E. Blair Leighton

A QUESTION  (Size 11½x9 inches.)

200 *Japan Proofs* — 18 00
200 *India Proofs* — *all sold*

HOURS OF IDLENESS  (Size 10x16 inches.)

50 *Japan Proofs* — 18 00
100 *India Proofs* — 12 00

TWO STRINGS  (Size 11½x9 inches.)

200 *Japan Proofs* — 18 00
200 *India Proofs* — *all sold*

SUNDAY MORNING  (Size 11½x8½ inches.)

50 *Japan Proofs* — 15 00
100 *India Proofs* — 12 00

Copyright 1891, by Photographische Gesellschaft.

A. J. ELSLEY—GOOD BYE.

## Sir Frederick Leighton

CAPTIVE ANDROMACHE    (Size 18x36 inches.)

    250 *India Proofs* .     .     .     .        *all sold*

BATH OF PSYCHE    (Size 22x8 inches.)

    100 *Japan Proofs*     .     .        *all sold*
    150 *India Proofs* .     .        *all sold*

GREEK GIRLS PLAYING AT BALL    (Size 18x30½ inches.)

    100 *Japan Proofs*     .        .        $40 00
    200 *India Proofs* .     .        .        30 00

PERSEUS AND ANDROMEDA    (Size 29x16 inches.)

    150 *Japan Proofs*        36 00
    150 *India Proofs* .        24 00

AT THE FOUNTAIN    (Size 20½x11½ inches.)

    150 *Japan Proofs*     .     .        24 00
    250 *India Proofs* .     .        18 00

## G. D. Leslie

ROSE QUEEN    (Size 20½x15 inches.)

    100 *India Proofs* .     .        .        18 00

# W. Logsdail

ST. MARTIN-IN-THE-FIELD   (Size 19½x16 inches.)

    50 *Japan Proofs* .               $20 00
    100 *India Proofs* .              15 00

# E. Long

THE SQUIRE'S DAUGHTER   (Size 20½x14½ inches.)

    75 *Japan Proofs* .             20 00
    150 *India Proofs* .             15 00

# C. F. Lowcock

A LOVE-LETTER   (Size 9½x15½ inches.)

    100 *Japan Proofs*             15 00
    100 *India Proofs* .            10 00

# Marie Seymour Lucas

WE ARE BUT LITTLE CHILDREN WEAK   (Size 10x16 inches.)

    100 *India Proofs* .            12 00

# H. W. Mesdag

LE MATIN
LE RETOUR DES BARQUES DE PÊCHEURS  } (Size 20x16 inches.)

    100 *India Proofs of each*          15 00

# Sir John Millais

THE VALE OF REST   (Size 16⅞x28⅞ inches.)

    100 *Japan Proofs*            40 00
    100 *India Proofs* .            30 00

# H. Moore

THE CLEARNESS AFTER RAIN   (Size 20x29⅞ inches.)

    100 *India Proofs* .          *all sold*

WRECKED AT THE HARBOR'S MOUTH   (Size 17½x30 inches.)

    150 *India Proofs* .          15 00

# Fr. Morgan

A HEAVY LOAD
THE TIRED GLEANERS  } (Size 22½x15 inches.)

    150 *India Proofs of each*       *all sold*

A GENTLE REMINDER   (Size 11x13 inches.)

    100 *India Proofs* .          *all sold*

WATCHING AND WAITING   (Size 16x20 inches.)

    150 *India Proofs* .            15 00

## L. C. Nightingale

A FORETASTE OF SUMMER    (Size 10½x20½ inches.)

     50 *Japan Proofs* .      .    .      .       *all sold*
     100 *India Proofs* .     .    .      .       *all sold*

A CORNER OF THE LAKE    (Size 10½x20⅜ inches.)

     50 *Japan Proofs* .        .    .      $24 00
     100 *India Proofs* .      .    .       18 00

DAWN OF SUMMER    (In progress.)

Copyright 1893, by Photographische Gesellschaft.

TH. BLINKS.—A DAY WITH THE OAKLEY.   "HARK AWAY."

## R. Poetzelberger

OLD SONGS    (Size 13x20 inches.)
     200 *India Proofs* .             12 00

## Edw. J. Poynter

A CORNER IN THE MARKET-PLACE    (Size 15x15 inches.)
     150 *India Proofs* .      .    .    .      *all sold*

DIADUMENE    (Size 20x12 inches.)
     100 *India Proofs* .          *all sold*

A VISIT TO ÆSCULAPIUS    (Size 19½x29 inches.)
     100 *Japan Proofs*    .    .    .      40 00
     175 *India Proofs* .    .      .      30 00

## V. C. Prinsep

FIRST AWAKENING OF EVE   (Size 16x19 inches.)
75 *India Proofs* .                          .              $15 00

## Henrietta Rae

A NYMPH   (Size 21x13½ inches)
75 *India Proofs* .                                   *all sold*

SPRING FLOWERS   (Size 9x13 inches.)
150 *India Proofs* .       .      .                     6 00

## Rafael

SISTINE MADONNA.   *The first gravure published after the
masterpiece* (Size 35x26 inches.)
Proofs *before letters on India Paper* .             36 00

## Gustav Richter

QUEEN LOUISE   (Size 35½x22 inches.)
*Proofs before letters on India Paper*               36 00

## W. Dendy Sadler

CHORUS   (Size 23½x30 inches.)
50 *Japan Proofs*                              45 00
250 *India Proofs*                             36 00

## J. Sant

LITTLE STELLA   (Size 18x15 inches.)
75 *India Proofs* .                            15 00

## Solomon J. Solomon

THE JUDGMENT OF PARIS   (Size 25x17 inches.)
250 *India Proofs*        .        .          24 00

NARCISSUS   (In progress.)

## H. Sperling

THE FIVE SENSES   (Size 18x37 inches.)
200 *India Proofs*        .     .             24 00

## W. Reynold Stephens

SUMMER   (Size 14½x28½ inches.)
200 *India Proofs* .                          30 00

## J. L. Stewart

A BAPTISM.

A BAPTISM (Size 19½x29.)

200 *India proofs*                                $36 00

Mr. Stewart is the son of American parents, but was born in Paris, where he has always lived and worked.  In his adopted country, and amid the swarm of clever artists that crowd the capital, he has earned a place by himself as the accomplished painter of the amusements and social functions of the *American colony*—that fashionable world within the world of Paris, whose doings add so much to the gayety of nations.  His "Hunt Ball," and his "Five O'clock Tea," have made his name familiar to the public on both sides the water, and in the present picture, his latest work, he will no doubt continue to please those to whom his former pictures have so successfully appealed.   Here are the same naturalness in the attitudes, the same accuracy, without pettiness, in the details, and the modern curiosity about personalities is pleasantly excited by the assurance that all the *dramatic personæ* of this domestic scene are portraits of people who are conspicuous members of this gilded world.

## Marcus Stone

IN LOVE (Size 20x30 inches.)
200 *India Proofs* — *all sold*

THE RETURN OF THE LOVER (Size 23x11½ inches.)
150 *India Proofs* . $18 00

BRIGHT SUMMER (Size 19½x12 inches.)
125 *Japan Proofs* . 24 00
125 *India Proofs* 18 00

## J. M. Strudwick

ELAINE (Size 21x15 inches.)
100 *Japan Proofs* 20 00
100 *India Proofs* 15 00

## Wm. Strutt

WATCHING FOR STRAGGLERS (Size 11⅜x20½ inches.)
50 *India Proofs* . . . . 18 00

## Paul Thumann

ART WINS THE HEART (Size 20x15½ inches.)
225 *Japan Proofs* . . . . 20 00
175 *India Proofs* . . . . 15 00

## W. H. Trood

BREAKFAST (Size 14x21 inches.)
150 *India Proofs* . 15 00

## S. E. Waller

THE RUINED SANCTUARY (Size 21x15½ inches.)
350 *India Proofs* . . . . 15 00

## E. A. Waterlow

THE NURSERY (Size 13⅞x21 inches.)
50 *India Proofs* . . 18 00

## J. Haynes Williams

THE MINIATURE (Size 10½x13¾ inches.)
75 *India Proofs* . . . . *all sold*

NO THOROUGHFARE (Size 22x15 inches.)
100 *India Proofs* . . . . $18 00

## C. Muennenberg

WOOING    (Size 21x12½ inches.)

     50 *Japan Proofs*            .          $24 00

     50 *India Proofs*                         18 00

WM. STRUTT.—WATCHING FOR STRAGGLERS.

# FACSIMILE GRAVURES IN COLORS.

The demand for good reproductions in colors, from paintings, has always been a loud one. The cheaper forms of this work, however, as oleographs, lithographs, etc., could not satisfy any but a very modest artistic taste. Since the rapid progress of reproductive art made by the invention of photography and kindred methods, it has been a desirable problem to produce a superior process for coloring in combination with the above. While the results in the line of photography in colors obtained hitherto are no more than interesting experiments, we have devoted special study to a process, which, while rendering the colors of the original painting as faithfully as possible, does also equal justice to the delicate softness of tints and to the richness of every detail of the qualities of our Photographs and Gravures.

Our Facsimile Gravures in colors are the result of this labor. They are made by hand in combination with our Gravure-process, and *printed from one plate* into which the colors are rubbed. They will be found very satisfactory specimens of really artistic reproductions in colors in the sense above pointed out.

# II.

## FACSIMILE GRAVURES IN COLORS.

**Hardy, Heywood.** Rotten Row.

11½ × 21 inches. $18.00

**Hernandez, Daniel.** Winter. (Fancy subject.)

10 × 7 inches. 6.00

*The Original of this picture, which has been exhibited with an enormous success in different large cities of this country, is in the possession of the Berlin Photographic Co.*

*For photographic editions see Part III.*

HOFMANN—CHRIST IN GETHSEMANE.

**Hofmann, H.** Christ in Gethsemane.

21 × 15 inches. 15.00

**Kaemmerer, F. H.** The Return.

20 × 14 inches. 15.00

**Müller, Carl.** St. Anne with Little Mary.

19 X 9 inches. } Companions,
each          $16.00

St. Joseph with Jesus Child.

19 X 9 inches.

**Perez, A.** En Excursion.

14 X 10 inches.          12.00

— L' Arrivée.

10 X 14 inches.          12.00

— La Rencontre.

10 X 7 inches. } Companions,
each          6.00

— Au Jardin.

10 X 7 inches.

**De Schryver, L.** Street Scene in Paris (Avenue du Bois).

8 X 9½ inches.          6.00

**Thumann, Paul.** Art Wins the Heart.

20 X 15 inches.          15.00

PEREZ, EN EXCURSION.

# III.

## PHOTOGRAPHS AND GRAVURE PRINTS

FROM THE ORIGINALS BY MODERN MASTERS, AND A SELECTED NUMBER
FROM DRAWINGS AFTER CLASSICAL PICTURES, ARRANGED ALPHA-
BETICALLY ACCORDING TO THE NAMES OF THE ARTISTS.

The reproductions mentioned in this part are principally such of *modern paintings*.

The classical pictures represented therein and marked by an "a" added to the number are but a small selection of prominent works in European Galleries. They are, however, not taken from the originals themselves, but from highly finished drawings made after them. A list of our reproductions after old masters, *taken directly from the originals*, will be found in Part V.

## PHOTOGRAPHS.

Most of the photographs are published in different sizes, indicated by the letters *e, n, i, r, f*, after each title, as follows :

| | | | | | |
|---|---|---|---|---|---|
| $e$ = Extra, size of mount | $35\frac{1}{2}$x47 inches | . . . . | Price, | $15 | 00 |
| $n$ = Normal, size " | $31\frac{1}{2}$x43 " | . . . . . | " | 10 | 00 |
| $i$ = Imperial, size " | 26 x$33\frac{1}{2}$ " | . . . . . | " | 4 | 00 |
| $r$ = Royal, size " | $19\frac{1}{2}$x$25\frac{1}{2}$ " | . . . . . | " | 3 | 00 |
| $f$ = Folio, size either mounted as *Boudoir Cards on black cardboard*, size about 8x10 inches | . . . . | | " | 1 | 00 |
| Or as *Folio on India Paper* 15x20 inches | . . | | " | 1 | 00 |

## GRAVURES.

We beg to call special attention to the Gravure editions of pictures mentioned in this part.

The invention of the Gravure (also called Photo- or Helio-Gravure) is considered one of the most important improvements in the line of photographic reproduction. The process is based upon transferring the photograph on a copper plate, which is then etched and impressions made from it in the same way as from an engraving plate. This method has been justly characterized as a very successful combination of both a good photograph and engraving.

*We publish every gravure in one size only, of which we give the dimensions of the plate (not of the mount) and the price after each number.*

# III.

## PHOTOGRAPHS AND GRAVURE PRINTS

ARRANGED

## ALPHABETICALLY ACCORDING TO THE NAMES OF THE ARTISTS.

| No. | ARTIST AND TITLE. | Photographs Sizes.* | | Gravures. Size. | Price. |
|---|---|---|---|---|---|
| 1301 | **Achenbach, Andreas.** Ostende | | f | | |
| 2003 | — Moonlight Night | i | f | 15x20 | $5 |
| 1116 | **Achenbach, Oswald.** Marketplace in Amalfi | i | f | | |
| 1120 | **Adam, Fr.** Retreat of the French in Russia, 1812 | | f | | |
| 1121 | — The Cavalry Engagement near Floing in the Battle of Sedan | e i | f | | |
| 2221 | **Adams, Douglas.** Woodcock Shooting | | | 12½x23 | 5 |
| 2249 | — The Salmon Poacher | | | 12½x23 | 5 |
| 2250 | — Golden Autumn | | | 12x23 | 5 |
| 1343 | **Alma-Tadema, Laura.** In Winter | | f | | |
| 1344 | — The Sisters | | f | | |
| 1555 | — Bible Lesson | | f | | |
| 2036 | — Nothing Venture, Nothing Have | r | f | 10x16 | 3 |
| 2063 | — Battledoor and Shuttlecock | r | f | 13x10 | 3 |
| 844 | **Alma-Tadema, Lorenz.** An Audience at the Palace of Agrippa | i r | f | | |
| 917 | — A Sculptor's Model | e i | f | | |
| 959 | — Young Girl | | f | | |
| 1161 | — A Hearty Welcome | i | f | | |
| 1276 | — A Portrait | | f | | |
| 1277 | — " Ave Cæsar ! Io Saturnalia " | i | f | | |
| 1342 | — Sappho, (Companion to No. 1672) | e i | f | 11x19½ | 5 |
| 1434 | — Portrait of Hans Richter | i | f | | |
| 1435 | — Barnay as Mark Anthony | i | f | | |
| 1549 | — Portrait of my Daughter | | f | | |
| 1550 | — Idyl | | f | | |
| 1570 | — Portrait of the Singer Georg Henschel | | f | | |
| 1603 | — An Old Story | r | f | 6x12 | 3 |
| 1672 | — A Reading from Homer. (Comp. to No. 1342 and 2208) | e i | f | 16x33 | 12 |
| 1798 | — Anthony and Cleopatra | e i | f | | |
| 1899 | — At the Shrine of Venus | e i | f | 21x27 | 12 |
| 2200 | — Love in Idleness (Companion to No. 1672) | e i | f | 17x33 | 12 |
| 2226 | — An Earthly Paradise | e i | f | 16x29 | 12 |
| 2329 | — Portrait of Paderewski (for Artist's Proofs see Part I.) | r | f | 10x13. | 3 |
| 2328 | — Unconscious Rivals (for Artist's Proofs see Part I.) | i | f | 14½x20 | 5 |
| 2349 | — In My Studio (for Artist's Proofs see Part I.) | e | f | | |
| 356 | **Amberg, W.** Oracle of Love | i r | | | |
| 460 | — Returning from the Matins | r | f | | |
| 461 | — Dressing for the Matinée | i r | | | |
| 462 | — Welcome | i r | | | |
| 586 | — At Sea | i r | | | |
| 733 | — Quite Absorbed | r | f | | |
| 814 | — Hero, *Grecian Female Figure.* (Companion to No. 1200) | i r | f | | |
| 815 | — A Severe Lecture | r | | | |
| 889 | — A Young Noble Lady | | f | | |
| 890 | — In Summer | | f | | |
| 1025 | — Sour Grapes | | f | | |
| 1126 | — Up Hill ⎫ Companions | | f | | |
| 1127 | — Down Dale ⎭ | | f | | |

* *The letters e u i r f indicate the sizes in which the photos are published. For prices see p. 20.*

21

| No. | ARTIST AND TITLE | Photographs Sizes.* | Gravures, Size. Price. |
|---|---|---|---|
| 1128 | **Amberg, W.** Justification. (Companion to No. 1225) | f | |
| 1209 | — Sappho, *Grecian Female Figure.* (Companion to No. 814) | i r f | |
| 1225 | — En Passant. (Companion to No. 1128) | f | |
| 1226 | — Sorrowful Thoughts | f | |
| 1305 | — An Echo | f | |
| 1329 | — The Parson's Cook | f | |
| 1339 | — In Autumn (Young Woman) | f | |
| 1340 | — An Uninvited Guest | f | |
| 1389 | — Bear Destiny's Decree (Companion to No. 1441) | f | |
| 1390 | — Misdroy | f | |
| 1441 | — Fickle Favor (Companion to No. 1389) | f | |
| 1515 | — Meeting in the Woods (Companion to 1540) | f | |
| 1516 | — Steamer in Sight | i | |
| 1517 | — The Waitress of the Inn | f | |
| 1538 | — The Country-joiner | f | |
| 1539 | — In the Loam-pit | f | |
| 1540 | — At the Forester's House (Companion to 1515) | f | |
| 1576 | — Marion (Study-head) | i | |
| 1577 | — Solitude (Young woman) | f | |
| 1585 | — Resting | f | |
| 1601 | — A Letter from Him | f | |
| 1602 | — The Défilé | f | |
| 1611 | — Good Morning (Study-head) | f | |
| | **Amberg Album.** See Part VI. | | |
| 1932 | **Andreotti, F.** A Cup of Coffee | f | |
| 2062 | — Teresa (Study-head) | f | |
| 2080 | — In the Park | i | 13x20 $5 |
| 93 | **Angeli, H. v.** Honor Avenged | n i r f | |
| 376 | — Absolution Refused | c i r | |
| 618 | — Emperor Frederick (In the uniform of Curassiers) | c i r f | |
| 619 | — Empress Frederick (Companion to No. 618) | c i r f | |
| 667 | — Emperor William I. (Companion to No. 618) | c i r f | |
| 841 | — Mary, Duchess of Edinburgh | i r | |
| 842 | — Prince Frederick Charles (Companion to 618 u. 667) | c i r f | |
| 997 | — Princess Charlotte of Meiningen | i f | |
| 1102 | — Ludwig IV., Grand-duke of Hesse | i f | |
| 1103 | — Alice, Grand-duchess of Hesse (Companion to No. 1102) | c i f | |
| 1210 | — Fieldmarshall von Manteuffel | i f | |
| 1318 | — Emperor William II. when Prince of Prussia | i f | |
| 1319 | — Empress Augusta Victoria, when Princess William | i f | |
| 1617 | — Emperor Frederick (Curassier uniform, Bust) | i f | 18x14½ 5 |
| 2342 | **Archer, James.** "From the Ballad of Sir Patrick Spens" | i f | |
| 817 | **Arnim, v.** The last Moments of King Henry IV. of England | i r f | |
| 1861 | **Assmus, R.** Departure from Säkkingen | c i f | 12x21 5 |
| 2029 | — At the Green-Leaf Inn | i f | |
| 2215 | — Arrival at Säkkingen | c i f | 12x21 5 |
| 2000 | **Aubert, J.** Les Voisins de Campagne | i f | 20½x15 5 |
| 2320 | **Axilette, A.** Arthémise | n i f | 20x29½ 12 |
| 2240 | **Ballavoine, I.** Le Printemps | i f | 20x14 5 |
| 1963 | **Barison, G.** Rendezvous | r f | |
| 1964 | — Proposing | f | |
| 616 | **Barth, F.** Choosing the Caskets | n i r f | 20x29½ 12 |
| 714 | — The God of Wine | i r | |
| 833 | — Tasso and the Two Eleonores | i r | |
| 3a | **Battoni.** Penitent Magdalen. (Dresden) | c i f | |
| 188 | **Becker, C.** Venetian Lady | n i r f | |
| 298 | — Albrecht Dürer in Venice | c i f | 28x34 15 |
| 428 | — The Alderman's Toilet | i r f | |
| 530 | — Street Musicians | i r | |
| 531 | — Venetian Lady | i r | |
| 601 | — The Lute-player | r | |
| 656 | — Gentlewoman | r | |

* *The letters c n i r f indicate the sizes in which the photos are published. For prices see p. 20.*

1672. ALMA-TADEMA.—A READING FROM HOMER.

| No. | ARTIST AND TITLE. | Photographs Sizes.* | Gravures Size. Price. |
|---|---|---|---|
| 666 | **Becker, C.** The Marriage of Figaro . | i r f | |
| 678 | — Viola and Olivia . | i r f | |
| 689 | — Dolores (Study-head) ⎱ Companions | r | |
| 690 | — Lady Playing Lute ⎰ | i r f | |
| 799 | — Charles V. at Fugger's . | e i r f | |
| 820 | — Birthday-morning . | r | |
| 821 | — Mandolinata . | i r | |
| 822 | — A Nurse . | r | |
| 825 | — Ulrich von Hutten being crowned with Laurel by Emperor Maximilian at Augsburg . | e i r f | |
| 826 | — Spanish Lady . | i r | |
| 827 | — Study-head ⎱ Companions | i r | |
| 849 | — Study-head ⎰ | i r | |
| 968 | — A Venetian Embassy begging Emperor Maximilian for Peace after the Capture of Verona . | e i f | |
| 969 | — A Girl from the Spree-Forest . | i f | |
| 970 | — A Cup of Coffee (Study-head) . | i f | |
| 975 | — Welcome Guests . | i f | |
| 976 | — Toilet for the Walk . | i f | |
| 1024 | — Italian Girl in Church . | i f | |
| 1093 | — Rivals . | i f | |
| 1136 | — Happy Return . | i f | |
| 1158 | — A Reminiscence of Venice (Young lady) . | i f | |
| 1162 | — Starting for the Hunt . | f | |
| 1168 | — Study-head ⎱ Companions | i f | |
| 1169 | — Study-head ⎰ | i f | |
| 1202 | — Expectation . | i f | |
| 1203 | — Study-head . | f | |
| 1252 | — Othello narrating his Adventures to Desdemona and her father Brabantio. (Companions Nos. 1678, 1490) | e i f | 27x31¼ $15 |
| 1377 | — The Offended Lover . | i f | |
| 1378 | — Ave Maria . ⎱ Companions | e i f | |
| 1384 | — A Petitioner before the Doge of Venice ⎰ | e i f | |
| 1490 | — Romeo and Juliet at the Friar's. (Companion to No. 1678, 1252) . | e i f | 29x32 15 |
| 1575 | — Carnival in Venice. (Companion to No. 1678) . | e i f | |
| 1613 | — Faust and Margaret . | e i f | 18½x14½ 5 |

* The letters e n i r f indicate the sizes in which the photos are published. For prices see p. 20.

| N. | ARTIST AND TITLE. | Photographs Sizes.* | | Gravures, Size. Price. | |
|---|---|---|---|---|---|
| 1578 | **Becker, C.** Othello's Defence before the Duke and Senators of Venice against Brabantio's accusation. (Companion to Nos. 1252, 1490, 1575) | | c i | f | 25½x33½ | 15 |
| 1679 | — A Venetian Romance . | | i | f | | |
| 1785 | — The newly found Statue of Apollo of Belvedere Viewed by Pope Julius II. and his contemporaries | | c i | f | 25x34 | 15 |
| 1952 | — A Great Temptation . | | i | f | | |
| 1953 | — After Reading the Will | | n i | f | | |
| 2095 | — In the Time of the Medici . | | c i | f | | |
| 2344 | — On the Balcony . | | i | f | | |
| | **Becker-Album.** See Part VI. | | | | |
| 2144 | **Beckert, P.** Portrait of Emperor William II. | | i | f | | |
| 2207 | — Portrait of Admiral v. d. Goltz | | i | f | | |
| 816 | **Beckmann, C.** Holiday-folks | | c i r | | | |
| 1194 | **Begas, A.** Midsummer | | | f | | |
| 1558 | — The Summer of Life . | | i | f | | |
| 1566 | — Pan and Nymphe | | | f | | |
| 1325 | **Begas, O.** Eve. (Companion to Graef, No. 1629) | | i | f | | |
| 1791 | **Behmer, F. H.** The Vision of the Novice . | | | f | | |
| 609 | **Benczûr Gyulà.** Louis XV. and the Countess Dubarry | | c i r | f | | |
| 410 | **Bendemann, E.** The Jews led into Babylonian Captivity | | c i r | f | | |
| 1282 | **Biermann, G.** Esther | | | f | | |
| 1453 | — At the Window . | | | f | | |
| 2184 | — Christ Ascending on High . | | i | f | | |
| 2185 | — Spring of Life (Female Bust) | | | f | | |
| 2260 | — Devotion | | r | f | | |
| 2204 | **Bisson, E.** La Fiancée | | i | f | 18½x14½ | 5 |
| 2237 | — Séraphine ⎱ Companions | | i | f | 20x14½ | 5 |
| 2238 | — Floréal ⎰ | | i | f | 20x14½ | 5 |
| 2272 | — L'Écho ⎱ Companions | | i | f | 20x14 | 5 |
| 2355 | — L'Attente ⎰ | | i | f | | |
| 2380 | — Satania | | i | f | | |
| 1905 | **Blaas, E. v.** Rosina . | | i | f | 20½x14 | 5 |
| 1913 | — Bianca ⎱ Companions | | r | f | | |
| 1914 | — Camilla ⎰ | | r | f | | |
| 1942 | — Marianna ⎱ Companions | | i | f | 20½x14 | 5 |
| 1943 | — Graziella ⎰ | | i | f | | |
| 1944 | — Angiolina . | | r | f | | |
| 1979 | — Giulietta . | | | f | | |
| 2176 | — A Gourmand | | i | f | 21x14½ | 5 |
| 2234 | — Punch and Judy . | | n i | f | 20x29 | 12 |
| 2361 | — The Wedding | | n i | f | | |
| 169 | **Bleibtreu, G.** Arrival of the Bavarians under Command of General von Hartmann before Paris . | | c r | f | | |
| 754 | — Capitulation of Sedan ⎱ Companions . | | c i r | | | |
| 755 | — Council of War at Versailles ⎰ | | c i r | | | |
| 805 | — Battle of Königgrätz . | | c i r | f | | |
| 1227 | — The Dying Heroes | | i | f | | |
| 1293 | — The Crownprince Albert of Saxony in the Battle of Gravelotte | | i | f | | |
| 1323 | — Episode from the Battle of Wörth | | c i | f | | |
| 1816 | — The Prussian Army landing at Alsen . | | i | f | | |
| 2259 | **Blinks, Th.** Partridge Shooting | | | f | 16x20 | 5 |
| 2263 | — A Fair Lead . | | i | f | 20x14 | 5 |
| 2264 | — Going Well . | | i | f | 20x14 | 5 |
| 2322 | — The Draw ⎱ | | i | f | 13x21 | 5 |
| 2323 | — Hark Away ⎰ A Day with the Oakley . | | i | f | 13x21 | 5 |
| 2324 | — Full Cry ⎱ For Artist's Proofs see Part I. | | i | f | 13x21 | 5 |
| 2325 | — The Finish ⎰ | | i | f | 13x21 | 5 |
| 1416 | **Blume, E.** A Shower in the Drawing-Room | | | f | | |
| 1422 | — A Pouting Model . | | i | f | | |
| 1684 | **Bochenek, J.** Immaculate Conception . | | i | f | | |
| 1118 | **Bochmann, G. v.** Wharf in Southern Holland . | | | f | | |

*The letters c n i r f indicate the sizes in which the photos are published. For prices see p. 20.*

| No. | ARTIST AND TITLE. | Photographs Sizes. * | Gravure Size. | z. |
|---|---|---|---|---|
| 2040 | **Bodenhausen, C. v.** First Love | n i | f | 21x14 $5 |
| 2228 | — Mother's Happiness | n i | f | 21x14 5 |
| | *Originals in possession of the Berlin Photographic Company.* | | | |
| 1091 | **Boecklin, A.** The Regions of Joy | i | f | |
| 130 | **Boeker, C.** In the Museum | i r | | |
| 571 | — The Extravagant Hotel-bill | i r | | |
| 1639 | — Your Health ! | i | f | |
| 1658 | — Morning Walk of the Princess | e i | f | |
| 2375 | **Bohrdt, H.** H. M. Yacht *Hohenzollern* | i | f | |
| 921 | **Bokelmann, L.** Before the Smash | e i | f | |
| 1173 | — Opening the Will | i | f | |
| 1356 | — The Arrest | e i | f | |
| 42a | **Bol.** Repose on the Flight into Egypt (Dresden) | | f | |
| 43a | — Jacob's Dream (Dresden) | | f | |

*For the assistance of persons who are not familiar with the names of the artists, there is given in PART IV. a classification of a selected number of popular subjects, arranged according to their titles, with a short explanation of the subjects.*

2238. BISSON.—FLORÉAL.

| | | | | |
|---|---|---|---|---|
| 168 | **Borckmann, A.** Mozart and Beethoven | } Com- panions { | i r f | |
| 271 | — Beethoven and the Rasumowsky Quartette | | i r f | |
| 561 | — Goethe in Sesenheim | | i r f | |
| 1144 | — A Dinner in Honor of Mozart at Schikaneder's | } Com- panions { | i f | |
| 1324 | — Mozart and his Sister before Maria Theresia | | i f | |
| 1509 | — In the Berlin Museum | | f | |
| 1702 | — The Philosopher of Sanssouci | } Companions { | f | |
| 1703 | — Frederick William I. in his Laboratory at Berlin | | f | |

* The letters e n i r f indicate the sizes in which the photos are published. For prices see p. 20.

| No. | ARTIST AND TITLE. | Photographs Sizes.* | Gravures. Size. Price. |
|---|---|---|---|
| 702 | **Böttcher, C. F.** Sunday on the Rhine | i r | |
| 2197 | **Bource, H.** Hercules and Omphale | i f | |
| 1371 | **Bracht, Eugen.** After Sundown at the Dead Sea ⎱ Companions | i f | |
| 1372 | — Moonlight Night in the Desert ⎰ | i f | |
| 1908 | **Brausewetter, O.** General York's Address to the Prussian Deputies on February 5th, 1813 | c i f | |
| 2139 | — Luther ⎱ Companions | i f | |
| 2140 | — Copernicus ⎰ | i f | |
| 2177 | — Christ on the Cross | c i f | |
| 1736 | **Bredt, F. M.** Arabian Lady Boating ⎱ Companions | i f | |
| 1763 | — Public Scribe in Tunis ⎰ | i f | |
| 2002 | — Arabian Bath for Women in Tunis ⎱ Companions | i f | |
| 2051 | — An Arabian Bathing-house for Women ⎰ | i f | |
| 2303 | — "Chopin" (fancy subject) | r f | |
| 903 | **Breitbach, C.** A Joyful Walk ⎱ Companions | i r f | |
| 904 | — A Sad Return ⎰ | i r f | |
| 1149 | — Children Fishing | f | |
| 1295 | — Holiday Morning in the Village Inn | i f | |
| 52 | **Bronzino.** Duchess Eleonore (Dresden) | f | |
| 1460 | **Buerck, H.** Sappho and Alcaeos | i f | |
| 1582 | **Bülow, P.** Emperor William II. in the uniform of his Hussars | c i f | |
| 1790 | — Emperor William II. in hunter's costume | i f | |
| 1823 | — Emperor William I. ⎱ Companions | i f | |
| 1834 | — Emperor Frederick ⎰ | c i f | |
| 1835 | — Emperor Frederick (Bust) | c i f | |
| 1855 | — Emperor William II. (Bust) | i f | |
| 1687 | **Calderon, Ph. H.** A Rose of Provence | i f | 19x 9 $5 |
| 2248 | **Calderon, W. F.** Orphans | i f | 10x20½ 5 |
| 170 | **Camphausen, W.** The Great Elector ⎱ Companions | c i r | |
| 234 | — Frederick the Great ⎰ Equestrian | c i r | |
| 318 | — Emperor William I. and his Generals ⎰ Portraits. | c i r | |
| 613 | — Emperor William I. (On horse-back) | c i r f | |
| 614 | — Frederick the Great at the Bier at Schwerin | c i r | |
| 615 | — Episode from the Battle at Rossbach | i r | |
| 756 | — Emperor William I. Entering Berlin in July, 1871, at the Head of his Victorious Army | c i r f | |
| 757 | — General Seydlitz (Equestrian Portrait) | i r f | |
| 784 | — Emperor Napoleon Conducted to Emperor William by Bismarck after the Battle of Sedan | c i r f | |
| 802 | — Düppel (Danish War, 1864) | i f | |
| 933 | — General Zieten (Equestrian Portrait) | i r f | |
| 948 | — Emperor William I. and his Paladins Before Paris, 1870 | c i f | |
| 949 | — Emperor William I. (Full figure) | i f | |
| 1043 | — The Great Elector in the Battle of Fehrbellin | i f | |
| 1051 | — Emperor Napoleon and Prince Bismarck Conferring Together After the Battle of Sedan | i f | |
| 1174 | — Frederick William I., King of Prussia (Equestrian Portrait) | c i f | |
| 1218 | — Emperor William I. and Crownprince Frederick William | i f | |
| 1304 | — Horsemen in Cromwell's Time | i f | |
| 1313 | — Head of a Gray Horse ⎱ Companions | i f | |
| 1314 | — Head of a Bay Horse ⎰ | i f | |
| 1360 | — Stag Hunt | i f | |
| 1381 | — Prince Bismarck Meets Napoleon III. after the Battle of Sedan | i f | |
| 1413 | — The Great Elector at the Battle of Fehrbellin | i f | |
| 1482 | — Emperor William I. | i f | |
| 1483 | — Emperor William I., Emperor Frederick and their Suite | i f | |
| 1535 | — Emperor William I. (Standing figure). | i f | |

*The letters e i r f indicate the sizes in which the photos are Published. For prices see p. 20.*

| N. | ARTIST AND TITLE. | Photographs Sizes. * | Gra. Size | N. rice. |
|---|---|---|---|---|
| 1547 | **Camphausen, W.** Revenge | i | | |
| 1560 | — Friedrich Haase, the Actor, as Lord Bolingbroke | r f | | |
| 1636 | — Maria Theresia (Equestrian Portrait) | i f | | |
| 1689 | — Emperor Frederick (Equestrian Portrait, oval) | i f | 16x16 | $5 |
| 1697 | — The Evening After the Battle of Leuthen | e i f | | |
| 1787 | — Tilsit, 1807 } Companions | ( f | | |
| 1788 | — Sedan, 1870 } | f f | | |
| 60a | **Canaletto.** The Marketplace of Pirna (Dresden) | f | | |
| 12a | **Caracci.** The Genius of Glory (Dresden) | f | | |
| 1828 | **Carrington, J. Yates.** Familiarity Breeds Contempt | r f | 16x10 | 3 |
| 2024 | **Carstens, J. V.** A Flower Girl | r f | | |
| 1976 | **Cecchi, A.** Il Racconto del Nonno (Grandfather's Story) | i f | | |
| 1820 | **Chelminski. J. v.** Lost Trail | i f | 16x19 | 5 |
| 1821 | — An Afternoon in Hyde Park | e i f | 23x35 | 15 |
| 1839 | — The Empress of Russia Fox Hunting | e i f | 24x35 | 15 |
| 1840 | — Part of above picture | e i f | | |
| 1841 | — Prince Leopold of Bavaria Reviewing the I. Cavalry Brigade | e i f | | |
| 2170 | **Chelmonski, J.** Hunting the Mountain Cock | i f | | |
| 2171 | — Frog Concert | f | | |
| 2172 | — Night | f | 7½x10 | 2 |
| 10a | **Cima da Conegliano** Christ (Dresden) | f | | |
| 2392 | **Cipolla, E.** A Present of Love | f | | |
| 2098 | **Commans, Fr. H.** The Mother of the Good Shepard | i f | | |

2263. BLINKS—"A FAIR LEAD."

*The letters e n i r f indicate the sizes in which the photos are published. For prices see p. 20.*

*To accommodate out-of-town customers, we are prepared to send selected SAMPLE COPIES IN SMALL SIZES ON APPROVAL. Where such selections are desired, we would request some information as to subjects, etc., preferred. Transportation charges both ways must be paid by the party ordering.*

| No. | ARTIST AND TITLE. | Photographs Sizes. * | Gravures. Size. Price. |
|---|---|---|---|
| 885 | Conrad, A. Pay Before You Leave | i r f | |
| 1028 | — Poultry Market | i f | |
| 1178 | — On the Alm | i f | |
| 1236 | — Scene in a Tyrolean Inn | i f | |
| 1980 | Conti, T. Happiness | e i f | |
| | Cornelius, P. v. The Four Horsemen in the Books of Revelations | | 19x15½ $5 |
| | — Cartoons of the Frescoes in the Glyptothek at Munich, and Cartoons of the Campo Santo, see Part VI. | | |
| 8a | Correggio. Penitent Magdalen (Dresden) | f | |
| 9a | — Madonna of St. George (Dresden) | n i f | |
| 63a | — The Holy Night (Dresden) | n i f | |
| 108a | — Jupiter and Antiope (Paris) | f | |
| 161a | — Io and Jupiter (Berlin) | e i f | |
| 162a | — Head of Io (Berlin) | f | |
| 166a | — Leda Bathing with Her Playmates | e i f | |
| 66a | Correggio's School. St. Margaret (Dresden) | f | |
| 2168 | Corregio, M. Spring | i f | 20x16 5 |
| 812 | Courten, A. de Two New Victims | i r f | |
| 1138 | — The Victor | i f | |
| 1373 | — At the Well | f | |
| 2147 | Cullin, J. Racing at Epsom Downs | n i f | 17x29 10 |
| 1474 | Czachorski, W. v. Hamlet and the Players | e i f | |
| 1607 | — A Question | i f | 12x18½ 5 |
| 1909 | Daelen, E. Rhinegold (Female head) | i f | |
| 1982 | — Cupid in Disgrace | f | |
| 937 | Dahl, H. In the Norwegian Highlands. (Figure of a girl) | f | |
| 1044 | — Too Late (Companion to No. 1427) | i f | |
| 1045 | — Evening in the Norwegian Highlands | f | |
| 1046 | — Fishermen Returning Home | f | |
| 1134 | — At the Mercy of the Waves | i f | |
| 1156 | — A Child of the Mountains (Companion to No. 1420) | i f | |
| 1205 | — On the Way to Church | i f | |
| 1213 | — On the Ice | i f | |
| 1219 | — The Return | i f | |
| 1248 | — The Extreme Unction | i f | |
| 1267 | — On the Shore | i f | |
| 1300 | — Fisherfolk Rowing to the Market | i f | |
| 1334 | — Critical Remarks (Companion to No. 1376) | i f | |
| 1368 | — Norwegian Fishing-boat | i f | |
| 1376 | — Female Attraction (Companion to No. 1334 and 1427) | i f | 11x19 5 |
| 1408 | — Young Ladies' Boarding-school on the Ice | e i f | |
| 1409 | — Hay-time in Norway | i f | |
| 1420 | — Norwegian Peasant-Girl (Companion to No. 1156) | i f | |
| 1427 | — Toll Paid First (Companion to 1044 and 1376) | i f | 12½x19 5 |
| 1499 | — Hunting Partridges | i f | |
| | Dahl-Album. See Part VI. | | |
| 751 | David, J. L. Bonaparte Crossing the Alps | e i r | |
| 466 | Defregger, F. Italian Beggars ⎱ Companions | e i r f | |
| 611 | — The Brothers ⎰ | e i r f | |
| 864 | — The Victors Returning Home | e i r f | |
| 2265 | — The New Pipe | i f | 19x14½ 5 |
| 1766 | Deger, E. The Crucifixion | r f | |
| 2052 | — Crucifixion ⎱ Companions | e i f | 21x12 5 |
| 2053 | — Madonna and Child ⎰ | e i f | 21x11 5 |
| 2069 | — Madonna | f | |
| 2070 | — Madonna (in the mountains) | f | |
| 2071 | — Christ's Entrance into Jerusalem | n i f | |
| 2088 | — St. Joseph | r f | |
| 2206 | — St. Sebastian | r f | |
| 2089 | — The Saviour's Heart | i r f | |
| 2113 | — Madonna and Child | i f | |
| 2124 | — The Ascension | f | |

* The letters e n i r f indicate the sizes in which the photos are published. For prices see p. 20.

| No. | ARTIST AND TITLE. | Photographs Sizes.* | Gravure Size. | Price. |
|---|---|---|---|---|
| 2125 | **Deger, E.** Last Judgment | f | | |
| 2126 | — Pouring Out of the Holy Ghost | f | | |
| 2127 | — Head of Christ | f | | |
| 2128 | — David | f | | |
| 2129 | — Adam and Eve at the Body of Abel | f | | |
| 1198 | **Deiker, C. F.** Before the Fight } Companions | i | f | |
| 1199 | — The Victor } | i | f | |
| 1200 | — Boar at Bay | | f | |
| 1454 | — Stag in Rutting-time | i | f | |
| 1455 | — Pointer and Setter } Companions. Another Com- | i | f | 14x19 $5 |
| 1526 | — Take Care, Doggy } panion: No. 1643 | i | f | 13½x19 5 |
| 1553 | — Hallali! | i | f | |
| 1643 | — Danger Ahead (Companions Nos. 1455 and 1526) | i | f | 13½x19 5 |
| 1644 | — After the Combat | i | f | |
| 1677 | — Boar Fighting (Companions No. 1695 and 1890) | i | f | 14x19 5 |
| 1694 | — Foxes at Home | i | f | 14½x19 5 |
| 1695 | — Boar Hunt (Companions No. 1677 and 1890) | i | f | 14x19 5 |
| 1768 | — Deer in Autumn | i | f | |
| 1769 | — Mountain-cock Calling | r | f | |
| 1890 | — Boars Fighting (Companions No. 1677 and 1695) | i | f | |
| 2266 | — Well Retrieved | i | f | 14x19 5 |
| 2369 | **Delort, Ch. E.** Le Départ | i | f | |
| 2378 | **Dettmann, L.** "Das Volkslied" | i | | |
| 1122 | **Deutsch, R. v.** The Rape of Helena | e i | f | |
| 1333 | — Penelope | i | f | |
| 2314 | **Dicksee, M.** Child Handel (for Artist's Proofs, see Part I.) | n i | f | 15½x21 5 |
| 2404 | — The First Audience (in progress) | | f | |
| 1382 | **Dieffenbach, A.** A Secret | i | f | |
| 1680 | — Diligence } Companions (Scenes of childhood) | i | f | 17x13 5 |
| 1681 | — Greediness } | i | f | 17x13 5 |
| 1848 | — Waiting for his Share | r | f | |
| 2225 | — Expectation | | f | |
| 1135 | **Dielitz, K.** Emperor Frederick (Full figure) | | f | |
| 1191 | — Prince Bismarck (Companion: Lenbach, No. 1616) | i | f | |
| 1274 | — A Fairy of the Alps (Companion: Spangenberg, No. 1152) | i | f | 19x13 5 |
| 1527 | — Air (Ride of the Valkyries) | i | f | 19x11 5 |
| 1528 | — Fire (Wotan's Farewell from Brunnhild) } Com- | e i | f | 19x11 5 |
| 1529 | — Water (The Rhine Daughters) } panions | i | f | |
| 1530 | — Earth (Siegfried Slaying the Dragon) | i | f | |
| 1781 | — Emperor William I. (Half figure) | e i | f | |
| 1782 | — Emperor William I. (Bust) | e i | f | |
| 1902 | — Bulgarian Girl | | f | |
| 1938 | — Old Friends | | f | |
| 1954 | — "Grace" | i | f | |
| 1872 | **Dietrich, A.** Come to Me All Ye Who Are Weary and Heavy Laden and I Will Give You Rest | i | f | 19x11 5 |
| 2181 | — The Crucifixion | e i | f | |
| 2286 | **Doerstling, E.** Kant's Philosophic Dinner Party | i | f | |
| 4a | **Dolci.** Christ Blessing the Bread (Dresden) | | f | |
| 150a | — St. Cecilia (Dresden) | e i | f | |
| 169a | — Mary Magdalen (Florence) | e i | f | |
| 111a | — Mater Dolorosa | i r | f | 16½x33 5 |
| 758 | **Donadini, E.** The Entry of Flora | n i r | | |
| 40a | **Dou.** The Hermit (Dresden) | | f | |
| 436 | **Douzette, L.** Mill by Moonlight } Companions | i | f | 15x21 5 |
| 1715 | — Moonlight Landscape } | i | f | 15x21 5 |
| 2074 | — The Silvery Moon | i | f | 20x15 5 |
| 2269 | **Dubufe fils, G.** Le Printemps | | f | 21x9 5 |
| 1115 | **Dücker, E.** Eventide on Rügen | | f | |
| 532 | **Dürer.** Christ on the Cross (Dresden) | | f | |
| 34a | **van Dyck.** Charles I., King of England } | e i | f | |
| 35a | — Henrietta Maria, Queen of England } Companions | | | |
| | (Dresden) } | e i | f | |

* The letters e n i r f indicate the sizes in which the photos are published. For prices see p. 20.

Copyright, 1893, by Photographische Gesellschaft.

2311.   H. SPERLING—SAVED.

| No. | ARTIST AND TITLE | Photographs Sizes | Gravures Size Price |
|---|---|---|---|
| 36a | **van Dyck.** The Children of Charles I. (Dresden) | c i | f |
| 178a | — Thomas de Carignan (Berlin) | | f |
| 157a | — Pieta (Berlin) | c i | f |
| 2270 | **Ebner, L.** The Dream (Female figure) | i | f |
| 1987 | **Ehrenberg, C.** The Nornes | i | f |
| 2112 | **Ehrlich, F.** The Prayer (Female figure) | i | |
| 582 | **Ekwall, Knut.** Ten Minutes for Dinner | i r | |
| 1665 | — Evening Hours | i | |
| 2281 | **Elsley, A. J.** A Dead Heat | | 21x13½ $5 |
| 2393 | — Good-bye (for Artist's Proof, see Part I.) | | |
| 1448 | **Encke, F.** Ariadne | i | f |
| 1237 | **Engel, Fr.** Fisher-wife | i | |
| 485 | **Epp, R.** The Uninvited Guest | i r | |
| 370 | **Erdmann, O.** Indiscretion | i r | |
| 425 | — The Love Letter | i r | |
| 1554 | — Trying to Steal a Kiss | i | f |
| 2405 | — Mandolin Player | i | |
| 1187 | **Ernst, O. v.** Riding to the Hounds | i | f |
| 1313 | — The Meet Before the Fox-Hunt | i | f |
| 743 | **Eybel, A.** The Great Elector in the Battle at Fehrbellin | c i | f |
| 1751 | **Falat, J.** Prince William of Prussia Bear-hunting | c i | f |
| 1946 | — Return of Emperor William II. from a Bear-hunt | c i | f |
| 1971 | — The Taming of the Shrew | i | f |
| 2104 | — Elk-hunting in Winter | i | f |
| 2105 | — Hunters Chasing the Bear with Spears | i | f |
| 2199 | — Emperor William at the Hunt | c i | f | 10x21 5 |
| 2137 | **Faléro.** Marina (*Female figure on the sea shore*) | i | f |
| 2390 | — La fumeuse d'opium | i | f |
| 2278 | **Fechner, H.** Expectation } Companions | i | f | 19½x14 5 |
| 2279 | — A Love Story } | i | f | 19½x14 5 |
| 2292 | **Fehr, F.** Friends | i | f |
| 1814 | **Ferrazzi, Luigi.** Mother's Delight | i | f |

* The letters c i r f indicate the sizes in which the photos are published. For prices see p. 20.

| No. | ARTIST AND TITLE. | Photographs sizes.* | | Gravure Size. |
|---|---|---|---|---|
| 644 | **Feuerbach, A.** The Symposium of Plato | | c i | f |
| 712 | — On the Sea-shore | | i r | f |
| 1969 | **Fildes, Luke.** La Zingarella (Gipsy-Girl) | | i | f | 20½x14 $5 |
| 2152 | — The Venetians | | c i | f | 29x20½ 12 |
| 2258 | **Firle, W.** Harmony | | u i | f | 26x23 12 |
| 2295 | — On Thee I Think | | i | f |
| 2039 | **Fisher, M.** November Evening | | i f | | 20½x14½ 5 |
| 1348 | **Fisher, S. M.** We Three | | i | f |
| 1349 | — A Moment of Idleness | | i | f |
| 2362 | — Southern Belle | | | f |
| 1622 | **Flamm, A.** View towards Cumæ | | i | f |
| 882 | **Fleischer, Ph.** Bitter Medicine | | r | f |
| 1507 | — Three Village Beauties | | i | f |
| 7a | **Francia.** Madonna and Child (Dresden) | | | f |
| 45 | **Freese, H.** Flying Stags | | i r | f | 11x20 5 |
| 883 | **Freyberg, C.** Prince Frederick Charles Arriving on the Battlefield of Vionville | | c i r | f |
| 884 | — Surrender of Metz | | c i r | f |
| 991 | — Stage-coach | | i | f |
| 1080 | — Count Lehndorff | | i | f |
| 1125 | — Emperor William I. | | | f |
| 1179 | — Before Le Mans | | i | f |
| 1296 | — Skirmish of the V. Armée Corps at Weissenburg | | c i | f |
| 1383 | — Prince Charles of Prussia (Equestrian portrait) | | i | f |
| 1387 | — Emperor Frederick (Equestrian Portrait) | | i | f |
| 1433 | — Spring Review at Potsdam | | c | |
| 1546 | — Prince Frederick Charles at Corny Castle Reviewing Conquered French Standards | | i | f |
| 1630 | — Frederick Francis, Grand Duke of Mecklenburg-Schwerin | | i | f |
| 1844 | — Emperor William I. | | i | f |
| 1873 | — Four-in-Hand (Portrait of Count Lehndorff) | | i | f |
| 2054 | — Emperor William II. (Equestrian portrait) | | c i | f |
| 1966 | **Fritze, M.** Emperor William II. | | i | f |
| 1569 | **Gabl, Alois.** Vaccination in a Village | | i | f |

COPYRIGHT, 1894,
BY PHOTOGRAPHISCHE GESELLSCHAFT.

2346. WÜNNENBERG—WOOING.

* The letters c n i r f indicate the sizes in which the photos are published. For price see p. 20.

| | ARTIST AND TITLE. | Photographs Sizes * | Gravures. Size. Price. |
|---|---|---|---|
| | Gallegos, J. Procession in Venice | i f | |
| | — La Confession | r f | |
| .5 | Gaupp, G. The Well | i r | |
| 510 | — Sacking a Monastery | i r | |
| 184 | Gebhardt, E. v. The Last Supper | e i r f | 22x34 $15 |
| 412 | — Christ Crucified | i r | |
| 426 | — The Crucifixion | e i r f | |
| 1005 | — Christ (Panel of an Altar) | i f | |
| 1298 | — Christ on the Waves | i f | |
| 1346 | — The Ascension | e i f | |
| 1379 | — Disputation | i f | |
| 1480 | — At Work | i f | |
| 1524 | — The Crucifixion | e i f | |
| 467 | Gebler, O. Art Critics | i r f | |
| 1060 | Geissler, W. " When the Cat 's Away," etc. | f | |
| 818 | Gentz, W. Crown-Prince Frederick Entering Jerusalem | e i r f | |
| 1224 | — A Reading from the Koran | f | |
| 1355 | — Festival in Memory of Rabbi Isaac Barchischat | f | |
| 1467 | — Idyl in Thebes | f | |
| 1784 | — Evening on the Nile | f | |
| 1951 | — Crown-Prince Frederick of Prussia Visiting the Tombs of the Califs Near Cairo | i f | |
| 1287 | Genzmer, B. The Black Man | f | |
| 2186 | Gessner, A. Psyche | r f | |
| 2187 | — Longing (Female figure) | r f | |
| 2180 | Gilli. Congress of Dogs for Emancipation from Masters | i f | 7½x21 5 |
| 6a | Gimignano. Madonna (Dresden) | f | |
| 2336 | Godward, J. W. At the Fountain | n i f | 23x15½ 5 |
| 2358 | — Yes or No? (for Artist's Proofs, see Part I.) | | |
| 1400 | Goldmann, O. A Secret | i f | |
| 2381 | Goodman, M. Hush! (for Artist's Proof, see Part I.) | | |
| 2119 | Gow, Andrew. After Waterloo | e i f | 24x34 15 |
| 1163 | Graef, G. Félicie (Companion to Kraus No. 1234) | i f | |
| 1279 | — Lady in the Costume of the 16th Century | i f | |
| 1355 | — Philomene | f | |
| 1629 | — Fairy Tale (Companion to Begas No. 1325) | i f | |
| 1721 | — Bianchina | f | |
| 1922 | — Ophelia | f | |
| 1929 | — For Love of Fatherland (Scene in the wars in 1813-15) | e i f | |
| 2350 | — Claire | f | |
| 1212 | Grass, A. The Nativity | i r f | |
| 1574 | — Madonna | i f | |
| 1586 | — The Immaculate Conception | i f | |
| 1628 | — Funeral in the Catacombs | i f | |
| 110a | Greuze. The Broken Pitcher (Paris) | e i r f | |
| 148a | — Head of a Girl (Berlin) | i f | |
| 184a | — Head of a Child (Berlin) | i f | |
| 1868 | Grosch, Cl. Farewell (Young lady) | i f | |
| 1188 | Grosse, Th. The Souls Entering the Land of Penance | i f | |
| 1638 | — The Judgment of Midas | i f | |
| 455 | Grützner, Ed. Brother Butler } Companions | i r f | |
| 456 | — The Wine-Taster } | i r f | |
| 474 | — In the Cloister's Cellar | e i r f | |
| 577 | — The Butler's Breakfast (Companion to No. 669) | i r | |
| 578 | — Self-Content (Companion to No. 628) | i r | |
| 627 | — The Hunter's Story (Companion to No. 650) | e i r f | 15½x19 5 |
| 628 | — The Favorite Mark (Companion to No. 578) | i r | |
| 650 | — The Maiden's Dilemma (Companion to No. 627) | e i r f | 15x19 5 |
| 669 | — Cook and Butler (Companion to No. 577) | i r | |
| 742 | — Music Lesson | i r | |
| 780 | — Time of Praying in the Monastery Inn | e i r f | |
| 782 | — A Friend of Birds | i r | |
| 853 | — Recreation (Companion to No. 982) | i r f | |

*The letters e n i r f indicate the sizes in which the photos are published. For prices see p. 20.*

2314. DICKSEE—CHILD HANDEL.

*The letters e n i r f indicate the sizes in which the photos are published. For prices see p. 20.

| No. | ARTIST AND TITLE. | Photographs Sizes.* | | Gravures. Size. Price. | |
|---|---|---|---|---|---|
| 1534 | Hafften, C. v.   A Wreck on a Northern Rocky Coast | i | f | | |
| 1545 | — Hamlet (Scene on the platform) Companion to No. 1627 | i | f | | |
| 1571 | — Coast of Northumberland ⎫ | | | | |
| 1572 | — The Road of Dieppe ⎬ Companions | i | f | | |
| 1573 | — Coast of Genoa ⎭ | i | f | | |
| 1605 | — Rising Moon on the Rhine | i | f | | |
| 1626 | — Coast of Ireland (Dunraven Castle) | i | f | | |
| 1627 | — Macbeth and the Witches (Companion to No. 1545) | i | f | | |
| 1632 | — Sappho and Her Companions (Landscape) | i | f | | |
| 1837 | — Hero (Landscape) | i | f | | |
| 1838 | — San Remo | i | f | | |
| 45a | Hals.   Portrait of a Man (Dresden) | | f | | |
| 2091 | Halswelle, Keeley.   Highlands and Islands | i | f | 12x21 | 85 |
| 2044 | Händler, P.   Between Love and Duty | i | f | | |
| 2132 | — Queen Louise of Prussia Visiting a Poor Family | i | f | | |
| 2389 | Hardy, Heywood.   Rotten Row (for facsimile gravures, see Part II). | | | | |
| 243 | Harrach, Graf.   In the Vineyards of Wörth ⎫ Companions ⎫ | i | r | | |
| 244 | — Outposts before Mount Valérien ⎬ ⎭ | i | r | | |
| 272 | — A Sea-King's Grave | i | r | | |
| 1159 | — The Denial of St. Peter | | f | | |
| 1177 | — Christmas-Eve | i | f | | |
| 1290 | — Evening at the Lake of Thun | | f | | |
| 2135 | — Moltke on His Death-Bed | r | f | | |
| 2076 | Hasse, F.   Just from School | | f | | |
| 2077 | Heichert, O.   Thy Word Giveth Light | | f | | |
| 1962 | Hein, Fr.   The Holy Legend of Gmünd | | f | | |
| 1591 | Hencke, A.   Stag on the Alert ⎫ Companions | i | f | | |
| 1592 | — Roes ⎭ | i | f | | |
| 2174 | — Evening in Autumn | i | f | 15x20 | 5 |
| 1940 | Hendrich, H.   Atlantis | | f | | |
| 1941 | — Voyage of the Vikings | | f | | |
| 2115 | Henley.   Suspense ⎫ Companions | i | f | 21x13 | 5 |
| 2116 | — Confidences ⎭ | i | f | 21x13 | 5 |
| 247 | Henneberg, R.   Reception of the Victors | | f | | |
| 248 | — Return of the Warriors | | f | | |
| 249 | — Little Cupids | r | f | | |
| 476 | — The Pet | r | | | |
| 479 | — Farewell ⎫ Companions | r | | | |
| 480 | — Taking Home the Bride ⎭ | r | | | |
| 800 | — The Hunt After Fortune | e i r f | | 17x33 | 12 |
| 2353 | Hernandez.   Winter.   (Published as facsimile gravure only.) See Part II. | | | | |
| 435 | Herpfer, C.   The Rose in Danger | i | r | | |
| 1633 | Hertel, A.   Scene on the Norwegian Coast | i | f | | |
| 1660 | — Mythological Landscape | i | f | | |
| 1661 | — Rest on the Flight into Egypt | i | f | | |
| 674 | Hertel, C.   Young Germany | i | r f | | |
| 1777 | Herterich, J. C.   Adagio ⎫ Companions | e i | f | 21x13 | 5 |
| 1862 | — Allegro ⎭ | e i | f | | |
| | *The originals are in possession of the Berlin Photographic Company.* | | | | |
| 489 | Herzog, H.   Waterfall in Norway | r | f | | |
| 1801 | Heydeck, J.   Queen Louise on her Flight from Königsberg to Memel in Winter 1807. | e i | | | |
| 1875 | Heydel, P.   At the Cobbler's | r | f | | |
| 2042 | — The Best Shot | r | f | | |
| 2043 | — Two Souls with But a Single Thought | | f | | |
| 2121 | — Spring | | f | | |
| 2160 | — The Lioness of San Marco (Female head) | | f | | |
| 2201 | — Violets | | f | | |
| 401 | Heyden, A. v.   Princess Clémence | i | r | | |
| 1228 | — The Rescue of Wittich | | f | | |
| 1415 | — The Vandals as Prisoners before Margrave Gero (963) | i | f | | |

* The letters e n i r f indicate the sizes in which the photos are published.   For prices see p. 70.

## III.—Photographs and Gravure Prints.

| No. | ARTIST AND TITLE | Photographs Sizes.* | Gravures. Size. Price. |
|---|---|---|---|
| 1207 | **Heyden, C.** Before the Ball | f | |
| 1645 | — Little Red Riding Hood | f | |
| 1667 | — In the Poultry-yard ⎱ Companions | s f | |
| 1668 | — Before the Sheep-fold ⎰ | f | |
| 1653 | **Heyden, Ch.** The Caricaturist | c | |
| 1700 | — My Mother-in-Law | c | |
| 1701 | — The Corporal | c | |
| 1876 | — A Dealer in Works of Art | c | |
| 1897 | — A Serenade | c | |
| 1907 | — In the Dress Circle | c | |
| 2005 | — The Student | c | |
| 2006 | — German Students | c | |
| 2111 | — Peasant Girl from the Black Forest | f | |
| 2235 | — Pierrette | f | |
| 1734 | **Heyser, F.** The Bird's Nest | f | |
| 1765 | — The Flower's Revenge | r f | |
| 120 | **Hiddemann, F.** Nemesis ⎱ Companions | s | i r |
| 121 | — The First Shave ⎰ | s | i r |
| 306 | — An Interrupted Winter Amusement | | r |
| 527 | — Examination in a Country School | | i r |
| 584 | — First Class Compartment ⎱ Companions | s | i r |
| 749 | — Third Class Compartment ⎰ | s | i r |
| 875 | — Prussian Enlisters at the Time of Frederick the Great | | i r f |
| 925 | — Westphalian Funeral | c i | f |
| 1132 | — Love ⎱ Companions | s | f |
| 1133 | — A Match of Convenience ⎰ | s | f |
| 1634 | — Little Red Riding Hood ⎱ Companions | s | f | 18x13 | 3½ |
| 1685 | — Cinderella ⎰ | s | f | 18x13 | 5 |
| 1879 | **Hirth du Frênes, R.** The Little Acrobat | | f | | 5 |
| 1880 | — Behind the Scenes | f | |
| 1974 | **Hoesslin, G. v.** Venetian Girl | | f i |

2123. THUMANN—ART WINS THE HEART.

We beg to call special attention to the FACSIMILE GRAVURES IN COLORS of this picture mentioned in Part II.

The original painting is in the possession of the Berlin Photographic Co., with a number of others as quoted on p. viii.

* The letters e n i r f indicate the sizes in which the photos are published. For prices see p. 20.

| No. | ARTIST AND TITLE. | Photographs Sizes * | | Gravures. Size. Price. | |
|---|---|---|---|---|---|
| 1975 | **Hoesslin, G. v.** Florentine Lady | | f | | |
| 2037 | **Hofmann, H.** Christ in the Garden of Gethsemane | e i | f | 21x15 | 85 |
| | (Published also as facsimile gravure, see Part II.) | | | | |
| | *The original is in possession of the Berlin Photographic Company.* | | | | |
| 54a | **Holbein, the Younger.** Madonna (Dresden) | e i | f | | |
| 62a | — Madonna [bust] (Dresden) | n i | f | | |
| | (For editions from the original in Darmstadt, see Part V.) | | | | |
| 55a | — Hubert Morett (Dresden) | | f | | |
| 1882 | **Holtzbecher, H.** Emperor William II. | n i | f | 18x15 | 5 |
| 1918 | — Empress Augusta Victoria (Companion to No. 1882) | i | f | | |
| 1269 | **Hübner, E.** Iphigenie | i | f | | |
| 803 | **Hübner, J.** The Golden Age | i r | f | | |
| 2252 | **Hulk, W. F.** Solitude | | | 20x12 | 5 |
| 274 | **Hünten, E.** The Hessian Division in the Battle of St. Privat | n i r | f | | |
| 652 | — The 11th Ulans Taking a French Battery at Loigny | i r | f | | |
| 677 | — The 53d Prussian Regiment at Colombey, 1870-71 | i r | | | |
| 723 | — The Staff of the 21st Division at Wörth | r | | | |
| 761 | — The 2d Squadron of Dragon-Guards Repulsing French Curassiers at Vionville | i r | f | | |
| 857 | — French Curassiers Attacking Elsasshausen (Wörth) | e i r | f | | |
| 1035 | — Outposts | | f | | |
| 1500 | — The Bremen Regiment in the Battle of Loigny | | f | | |
| 1658 | — The 39th Fusiliers at Gravelotte (Aug. 18, 1870) | i | f | | |
| 2131 | — Last Quarters of the Grand Duke of Hesse Before the War of 1870-71 | i | f | | |
| 537 | **Ittenbach, F.** Madonna Enthroned (Middle panel to the following two numbers) | i r | f | | |
| 538 | — St. Francis of Assisi } Companions | i | r f | | |
| 539 | — St. Elisabeth of Thuringia } | i | r f | | |
| 640 | — Ecce Agnus Dei } Companions | i | r f | | |
| 641 | — Mater Amabilis } | i | r f | | |
| 873 | — The Handkerchief of St. Veronica | i r | f | | |
| 879 | — Ecce Cor, Quod Mundum Tantopere Dilexit | i r | f | | |
| 927 | — The Holy Family in Egypt | i r | f | | |
| 991 | — Ego Dilecto Meo, et ad me Conversio Eius (Madonna and Child) | e i r | f | | |
| 1436 | — Maria Virgo } Companions | r | f | 8x10 | 2 |
| 1857 | — Infant Jesus } | r | f | 8x10 | 2 |
| | Other Companions: Sinkel, Nos. 1795, 1806. | | | | |
| 1858 | — John the Baptist | | f | | |
| 1860 | — The Holy Family | i | f | 19x14 | 5 |
| 2018 | — St. Hubert and St. Elisabeth } Companions | i | f | | |
| 2019 | — St. Frederick and St. Theresa } | i | f | | |
| 2020 | — St. Peter and St. John } Companions | i | f | | |
| 2021 | — St. Paul and St. Maurus } | i | f | | |
| 2064 | — Madonna | r | f | 9x16¼ | 3 |
| 2065 | — Madonna with Christ and St. John | | f | | |
| 2066 | — St. George } Companions | | f | | |
| 2067 | — St. Donat } | | f | | |
| 2068 | — Pilgrims Before Rome | | f | | |
| 2086 | — Mater Christi | n i | f | 20¼x14 | 5 |
| 2101 | — Queen of Heavens | r | f | | |
| 2102 | — St. Anne with Infant Mary } Companions | | f | 10x4 | 1 |
| 2103 | — St. Joseph with Infant Jesus } | | f | 10x4 | 1 |
| 1337 | **Jacobides, G.** Creusa | | | | |
| 2156 | **Jacobsen, S.** Landscape in Winter } Companions | i | f | 21x14 | 5 |
| 2157 | — Moonlight Night } | i | f | 21x14 | 5 |
| 1476 | **Jansen, P.** The Childhood of Bacchus | e i | f | | |
| 1696 | **Janssens, Jos.** Madonna and Child | | f | | |
| 1712 | **Jochmus, Harry.** Spring-time | r | f | | |
| 2333 | **Joy, G. W.** Truth (for Artist's Proofs, see Part I.) | n i | f | | |
| 1367 | **Kahler, C.** The Queen of the Season | | f | | |
| 1950 | **Kampf, A.** "Bon Soir, Messieurs" | e i | f | | |

* *The letters e n i r f indicate the sizes in which the photos are published. For prices see p. 20.*

## III.—Photographs and Gravure Prints.

*The original of No. 1999 is in the possession of the Berlin Photographic Company.*

COPYRIGHT, 1893, BY PHOTOGRAPHISCHE GESELLSCHAFT.

2303. BREDT—" CHOPIN."

* The letters e n i r f indicate the sizes in which the photos are published. For prices see p. 20.

| No. | ARTIST AND TITLE. | Photographs Sizes.* | Gravures. Size. Price. |
|---|---|---|---|
| 334 | Kindler, A.   Fandango | i r f | |
| 1181 | Kirberg, O.   A Victim of the Deep | i f | |
| 1182 | — The Interrupted Musician | f | |
| 1445 | — Fair in Holland | e i f | |
| 1565 | — A Serious Question | f | |
| 1809 | Kirchmayr, C.   Cupid and Psyche (Children) | i f | |
| 1927 | Klein, F. E.   The Last Signature of Emperor William I. | r f | |
| 1949 | — The Judgment of Paris | i f | |
| 1674 | Klenze, H. v.   A Lonely Death ⎫ | i f | |
| 1735 | — Victor and Victim ⎬ Companions | i f | |
| 1767 | — Cornered ⎭ | i f | |
| 1815 | — Black Game | r f | |
| 1824 | — Chamois and Bearded Eagle | i f | |
| 1486 | Klever, J. v.   Russian Forest | f | |
| 1487 | — Autumn | f | |
| 1488 | — In the Forest | f | |
| 1489 | — Falling Leaves | f | |
| 2154 | Klimsch, E.   A Crime | f | |
| 2162 | — Recreation | f | |
| 2326 | Klinger, M.   Pietà | i f | 15x21   5 |
| 240 | Knaus, L.   In Great Distress | n i r f | |
| 280 | — The Luncheon | e i r f | |
| 305 | — The Funeral | e i r f | |
| 397 | — His Royal Highness' Journey | e i r f | |
| 587 | — The Little Pirate ⎫ | n i r f | |
| 617 | — The Heir to the Farm ⎬ Companions | i r f | |
| 647 | — The Young Gamblers | n i r f | |
| 648 | — The Lectured Rivals | e i r f | |
| 811 | — The Holy Family | e i r f | 19x14   5 |
| 834 | — As the Old, So the Young (Companion to 2100) | e i r f | |
| 1000 | — The First Profit | i f | |
| 1100 | — Valuable Instruction | e i f | |
| 1180 | — Chimney-Sweep | i f | |
| 1220 | — Little Mother | f | |
| 1265 | — A Bad Customer | i f | |
| 1345 | — Rural Festival | e i f | |
| 1450 | — Study-Head | f | |
| 1583 | — Professor von Helmholtz | i f | |
| 1584 | — Professor Mommsen | f | |
| 1600 | — The Village Witch | e i f | |
| 1611 | — A Gipsy Team (Children) | n i f | 17x26   10 |
| 1711 | — I Can Wait | r f | |
| 1786 | — Charity | e i f | 15x21   5 |
| 1811 | — Sic Transit Gloria Mundi | r f | |
| 1887 | — The Artiste and Her Model | i f | 21x15   5 |
| 1888 | — Springtime | f | 8x9½   2 |
| 2100 | — A Pic-nic Party (Companion to No. 834) | e i f | 15x21   5 |
| 2221 | — A Fight Behind the Fence | n i f | 16x20½   5 |
| 2232 | — A Gipsy Girl | f | 9x7½   2 |
|  | Knaus-Album.   (See Part VI.) | | |
| 2239 | Knight, Ridgway.   She Has Lost Her Way | f | 19x15   5 |
| 409 | Knille, O.   Tannhäuser and Venus | e i r f | 16x16½   5 |
| 1369 | — The University of Paris in the XIIIth Century ⎫ | n | |
| 1370 | — The Humanist Welcome the Reformers ⎬ Companions. | n | |
| 1666 | — Weimar 1803 ⎭ | n | 10x15   10 |
| 1635 | — Venetian Lady | f | |
| 1850 | — "But Lo, I am With You Always Even Unto the End" | i f | |
| 1491 | Knöchl, H.   Scene from Schiller's Ballad "The Iron-mill" | f | |
| 2208 | — Foot Soldier | f | |
| 824 | Knorr, G.   In a Boarding-School for Young Ladies | i r f | |
| 1183 | — Out Into the Wide World | f | |
| 1330 | — Church Collection | f | |

\* The letters e n i r f indicate the sizes in which the photos are published.  For prices see p. ix.

| N | ARTIST AND TITLE | Photographs Sizes * | Gravures Size. | Price. |
|---|---|---|---|---|
| 716 | **Knüpfer, J.** The River's Bounty | i r | | |
| 1160 | **Koch, G.** A Critical Moment | i | f | |
| 1261 | — False Start | i | | |
| 1338 | — Hurdle-race | | f | |
| 1423 | — At the Watering Place | | f | |
| 1424 | — Biting Critics | | f | |
| 1425 | — The Sick Foal | | f | |
| 2256 | **Koch, H.** Sweethearts } Companions | i | f | 21x14 $5 |
| 2273 | — The Trysting Tree } | i | f | 20x15 5 |
| 2296 | **Koenig, H.** The Gardener's Daughter | r | f | |
| 2304 | — Lazy Land | r | f | |
| 411 | **Kolitz, L.** Transport of Prisoners near Metz | r | f | |
| 606 | — On the Retreat Near Le Mans | r | | |
| 1624 | — Scene From the Skirmish Near Vendôme | i | f | |
| 1789 | — Before Paris | i | f | |
| 2099 | **Koner, M.** Emperor William II. | c i | f | |
| 44a | **Koning.** The Hermit (Dresden) | c i | f | |
| 1391 | **Wierusz-Kowalski, A. v.** Sledge Riding in Lithuania During the Carnival | i | f | 11x19 5 |
| 1392 | — Starting for the Boar-hunt | i | f | |
| 1459 | — Circassians | i | f | |
| 1792 | — Across the Plains in Winter | i | f | |
| 1825 | — The Return from the Bear-hunt | i | f | |
| 1896 | — The Guests are Coming | i | f | |
| 974 | **Kraus, F.** Before the Ball | i | f | |
| 1195 | — Critics on Art | i | f | |
| 1196 | — Study-head | | f | |
| 1234 | — Bacchant Awaking (Companion to Graef No. 1163) | i | f | |
| 1235 | — Revery | | f | |
| 1322 | — Childish Amusement | i | f | |
| 1402 | — Renaissance | | f | |
| 1548 | — The Don Juan of the Court-yard | i | f | |
| 1804 | — Dolce Far Niente (Study-head) | r | f | |
| 1805 | — A Quiet Nap | | f | |
| 1859 | — Singing Lesson | i | f | |
| 1881 | — Nobody at Home | r | f | |
| 1889 | **Kray, W.** Pausias and His Flower-Girl | i | f | |
| 38 | **Kretzschmer, H.** In the Village Church } Companions | r | | |
| 75 | — The Village Doctor } | i r | | |
| 78 | — The Cat's Luncheon } Companions | i r | | |
| 132 | — Little Sweet-tooth } | i r | | |
| 300 | — The Village School | i r | | |
| 486 | — Caught! | i r | | |
| 518 | — Honeymoon | | | |
| 622 | — Grateful Patients | i r | f | |
| 660 | — Returning Home From School | i r | | |
| 692 | — Chambermaid's Vanity | r | | |
| 739 | — The First Cradle | r | | |
| 848 | — A Marriage at Gretna-Green in the Last Century | i r | f | |
| 1016 | — Sold Out (Figure of a child) } Com- | | f | |
| 1139 | — Un Bajacco, Signore (Figure of a child) } panions | i | f | |
| 1233 | — The Village Street | i | f | |
| 1464 | — The Milk is Boiling Over | | f | |
| 713 | **Kröner, Chr.** Deer in Winter | r | f | |
| 1119 | — Stags in Autumn | i | f | |
| 1312 | — Rutting Stag | i | f | |
| 1417 | — Breaking Through (Companion to No. 1686) | c i | f | 12x19 5 |
| 1595 | — Morning (Deer and Stags) } | i | f | 18½x14 5 |
| 1596 | — Evening } Companions | i | f | 18½x14 5 |
| 1604 | — Challenge (Stag) } | i | f | 18x14 5 |
| 1609 | — In Autumn (Deer in the mountains) } | i | f | 18½x14 5 |
| 1686 | — The Beat (Boar-hunt) (Companion to No. 1417) | c i | f | 12x19 5 |
| 2202 | — Stags Feeding | i | f | |

* The letters c n i r f indicate the sizes in which the photos are published. For prices see p. 20.

COPYRIGHT, 1893, BY PHOTOGRAPHISCHE GESELLSCHAFT.

*One of the reasons why our GRAV-URES are so highly favored by artists is that the tints chosen for printing are in each case adapted to the individual character of the painting.*

2327.　BLAIR-LEIGHTON—TWO STRINGS.

| No. | ARTIST AND TITLE. | Photo-grav. Sizes | Grav. Sizes | Price. |
|---|---|---|---|---|
| 2203 | **Kroner, Chr.**　A Winter Day | i f | | |
| 1726 | — Stag | i f | | |
| 2107 | — At Early Dawn | n i f | 22x29 | 8.12 |
| 2406 | — Hare Hunting | n i f | | |
| 2191 | **Kroyer, S.**　Session of the Committee of French Artists at Copenhagen | i f | 13x21 | 5 |
| 2299 | **Kuehl, G.**　Choristers | i f | | |
| 1924 | **Kuhnert, W.**　Arabian Spies Finding the Trail of a Caravan | i f | | |
| 934 | **Kuntz, G. A.**　In the Studio | i f | | |
| 935 | — A Roman Pilgrim-Girl | i f | | |
| 1058 | — The Confession | i f | | |
| 1059 | — All Saints' Day on the Capuchins' Cemetery | f | | |
| 629 | **Kurzbauer, E.**　The New Picture Book | i r f | | |
| 2031 | **Laasner, H.**　Blind Man's Buff | i f | | |
| 2013 | **Lauenstein, H.**　Beatrice ⎱ Companions | i f | | |
| 2014 | — Santa Lucia ⎰ | i f | | |
| 2341 | **Laupheimer, A.**　Flirtation | i f | | |
| 1811 | **Laurenti, C.**　Frons Animi Interpres | i f | | |
| 2268 | **Leader, B. W.**　Valley of the Llugwy | | 17x29 | 10 |
| 2354 | — Eventide (for Artist's Proofs, see Part I.) | | | |
| 2295 | **Leeke, F.**　Love's Service | i f | | |
| 1851 | **Lefler, H.**　A Dream | i f | 21x14 | 5 |
| 1985 | — Congratulation ⎱ Companions | i f | | |
| 1986 | — Dancing Lesson ⎰ | i f | | |
| 2300 | **Leibl, W.**　Grouse Shooting in Autumn | | 14½x20 | 5 |
| 2224 | **Leighton, Blair E.**　A Question | | 11½x9 | 3 |
| 2290 | — Hours of Idleness | | | |
| 2327 | — Two Strings | | 11½x9 | 3 |
| 2356 | — Sunday Morning (for Artist's Proofs, see Part I.) | | 11½x9 | 3 |

* The letters e n i r f indicate the sizes in which the photos are published.　For prices see p. 20.

| N | ARTIST AND TITLE. | Photographs | Gravure Prints |  |
|---|---|---|---|---|
| 1920 | **Leighton, Sir Fr.** Captive Andromache . | c i | 16½x35 8½2 |  |
| 2072 | — Greek Girls Playing at Ball | c i | 19x34 12 |  |
| 2096 | — Bath of Psyche . | n i | 21x7 5 |  |
| 2212 | — Perseus and Andromeda . | | 29x16 12 |  |
| 2254 | — At the Fountain . | | 20½x18 5 |  |
| 2383 | — Atalanta (for Artist's Proofs, see Part I.) | | |  |
| 1919 | **Leinweber, R.** An Arabian Song | c i | |  |
| 1640 | **Leisten, J.** New Music . | i | |  |
| 1871 | — A Concert at Richelieu's | i | |  |
| 1961 | — In the Waiting-room . | i | |  |
| 278 | **Lenbach, F. v.** R. Wagner } Companions | i | |  |
| 279 | — Fr. Liszt | i | |  |
| 1430 | — Prince Bismarck (Crayon-drawing) | c i | |  |
| 1615 | — Count Moltke (Half Length) Companion to No. 1664 . | i | |  |
| 1616 | — Count Moltke (Bust) Companion to No. 1817 . | i | 18x14 5 |  |
| 1664 | — Prince Bismarck (Half Length) Companion to No. 1615 | c i | |  |
| 1817 | — Prince Bismarck (Bust) Companion to No. 1616 . | c i | 18x14 5 |  |
| 1895 | — Charlotte, Hereditary Princess of Saxony-Meiningen . | i | |  |
| 2252 | **Leslie, G. D.** Rose Queen (for Artist's Proofs, see Part I.) | | 20½x15 5 |  |
| 804 | **Lessing, K. Fr.** Huss Before the Execution | c i | |  |
| 1303 | — Thunder-storm in the Eifel-Mountains | i | |  |
| 2045 | **Leu, A.** The Faraglioni near Capri } Companions | i | 14½x21½ 5 |  |
| 2046 | — Sunset near Capri | n i | 16x21 5 |  |
| 1752 | **Lieck, J.** Peasant Girl . | i | |  |
| 1753 | — Styrian Girl } Companions | i | |  |
| 1764 | — Lydia | i | |  |
| 2030 | — Joy of Life | i | |  |
| 2031 | — Happiness . | i | |  |
| 2117 | **Linderum.** The Monastic Flute-player | i | |  |
| 2134 | — Monk Reading . | i | |  |
| 2241 | **Lingner, O.** Springtime of Love | i | 21x13 5 |  |
| 2317 | — Roses | i | |  |
| 2316 | — Violets | i | |  |
| 1593 | **Lipps, F.** Spring (Child with flowers) } Companions | i | |  |
| 1696 | — Summertime (Child with flowers) | i | |  |
| 591 | **Liotard.** Vienna Chocolate-Girl (Dresden) | i | |  |
| 1461 | **Löwe, Marg.** Scene from the Merry Wives of Windsor . | c i | f |  |

2255. RAE—SPRING FLOWERS.

*Portfolios containing each 15 photographs of the best pictures of the following artists:*

L. KNAUS .
W. AMBERG .
E. GRÜTZNER .
B. VAUTIER . . . .
MEYER von BREMEN
HANS DAHL .
CARL BECKER . . . .
GUSTAV RICHTER at $14.

} at

} $10

each.

*For particulars see Part VI.*

* The letters c n l r f indicate the sizes in which the photos are published. For prices see p. 20.

| No. | ARTIST AND TITLE. | Photographs Sizes. * | Gravures Size. Price. |
|---|---|---|---|
| 2092 | **Logsdail, W.** St. Martin-in-the-Field | i f | 20x16 85 |
| 2090 | **Long, E.** The Squire's Daughter | i f | 20½x15 5 |
| 1223 | **Lonza, A.** The Interrupted Performance | i f | |
| 1690 | — An Interesting Story } Companions | ) i f | 18¾x12 5 |
| 1691 | — In the Park | ( i f | 18¾x12 5 |
| 29a | **Claude Lorrain.** The Flight Into Egypt (Dresden) | f | |
| 30a | — Coast of Sicily (Dresden) | f | |
| 186a | — Heroic Landscape (Berlin) | f | |
| 995 | **Lossow, H.** Confidences | f | |
| 1084 | — Interesting News | f | |
| 1145 | — The Milliner | i f | |
| 2153 | **Lowcock, C. F.** A Love-Letter | r f | 9x16 3 |
| 2339 | **Lucas, M. Seymour.** We Are But Little Children Weak (for Artist's Proofs, see Part I.) | r f | 10x16 3 |
| 1117 | **Ludwig, C.** The St. Gotthard's Pass | f | |
| 887 | **Lüben, A.** Young Talents | i r f | |
| 855 | — There 's a Fine Business | r f | |
| 1307 | — Wooing (Companion to No. 1443) | i f | |
| 1440 | — Political Discussions | f | |
| 1443 | — Trying to Make his Peace (Companion to No. 1307) | i f | |
| 1457 | — After the Christening | i f | |
| 1485 | — Rendezvous | i f | |
| 1722 | — The Morning Glass | i f | |
| 2008 | **Lybaert, Th.** Madonna | r f | |
| 1874 | **Mader, G.** Trio | f | |
| 1670 | **Maffei, G. v.** Attacked by Foxes | i f | |
| 1891 | — Spring | i f | |
| 1892 | — Summer } Companions | i f | |
| 1893 | — Autumn | i f | |
| 1894 | — Winter | i f | |
| 2082 | — A Wild Boar Track | i f | |
| 2083 | — Startled | i f | |
| 2084 | — Snipe | f | |
| 2307 | — A Corner of the Fens | r f | |
| 2308 | — The End of the Chase | i f | |
| 2309 | — Marauders | i f | |
| 2347 | — A Duel | i f | |
| 2253 | **Maillard, E.** Après la Tempête | | 15x29 10 |
| 607 | **Makart, H.** Abundantia (Bounty of the land) | n i r f | |
| 608 | — Abundantia (Bounty of the sea) | n i r f | |
| 960 | **Malchin, C.** A Flock of Sheep | f | |
| 1285 | — Winter Landscape (Motive from Thuringia) | f | |
| 1374 | — Evening in Autumn | e | |
| 1494 | — Winter Landscape (Motive from Mecklenburg) | f | |
| 2078 | — Coast Scene (Mecklenburg) | f | |
| 2079 | — Winter Landscape | f | |
| 2164 | — Winter Landscape | f | |
| 2165 | — Summer | f | |
| 2166 | — Summer Morning | f | |
| 2038 | **Maltzahn-Vidal, A. v.** In Good Keeping | f | |
| 1395 | **Marchetti, L.** The Bust of the Nabob | i f | 18x13 5 |
| 1481 | — The Winner of the Grand Prize in Paris | i f | |
| 1217 | **Marr, G.** Ahasver | i f | |
| 1637 | **Marshall, J.** The Sisters | f | |
| 1948 | **Matifas, L.** Winter Landscape | n i f | 18x29 10 |
| 610 | **Max, Gabriel.** Autumn | e i r f | |
| 1463 | — Homeward Bound | i f | |
| 1704 | — Magdalen | r f | |
| 1705 | — Angel Gabriel | f | |
| 1757 | — Magdalen } Companions (Study heads) | ) i r f | 17x14 5 |
| 1758 | — Mignon | ( i r f | 17x14 5 |
| 1883 | — Lost in Thought (Study head) | f | |
| 1884 | — Vestal Virgin (Study head) | f | |

* The letters e n i r f indicate the sizes in which the photos are published. For prices see p. 20.

| N. | ARTIST AND TITLE. | Photographs Size.* | Gravures Size. Price. |
|---|---|---|---|
| 1923 | **Max, Gabriel.** Lacrima (Tears) | . . *i* / | 19x15  $5 |
| 1933 | — Trust | *i* / | |
| 1972 | — Laura | / | |
| 1973 | — Beatrice | / | |
| 2049 | — Homesick | *i* / | 18x14  5 |
| 2130 | — Hope | *r* / | |
| 2340 | — Virgin Mary | *r* / | |
| 2352 | — Herodias | *r* / | |
| 2399 | — Phantom | / | |
| 47a | **van der Meer, J.** Young Woman Reading at a Window (Dresden) | / | |
| 182a | — Young Woman with Necklace of Pearls (Berlin) | / | |
| 2085 | **Meisel, E.** Sunshine | *i* / | |
| 2011 | **Melida, E.** First at the Rendezvous | *i* / | |
| 57a | **Mengs.** Portrait of Himself (Dresden) | / | |
| 58a | — Cupid (Dresden) | / | |
| 2175 | **Menshausen, Frieda.** Bound for Helgoland | *t* / | |
| 1 | **Menzel, A.** Concert at the Court of Frederick the Great | *e i r* / | 22x31½  15 |
| 1610 | — Rolling Mill | *i* / | |
| 2023 | **Menzler, W.** Expectation | *r* / | |
| 2213 | **Merritt, A. L.** When the World Was Young | *i* / | |
| 2182 | **Mesdag, H. W.** On the Coast Near Scheveningen at Flood-tide | *i* / | 16x20  5 |
| 2183 | — Sunrise | *t* / | 16x20  5 |
| 2242 | — Le Matin | *i* Compan- { | 20x16  5 |
| 2243 | — Le Retour Des Barques de Pêcheurs | } ions *r* | 20x16  5 |
| 2010 | **Metzmacher, C.** En Arrêt | *i* / | 20½x16  5 |
| 1205 | **Meyer, E. L.** After a Restless Night | / | |
| 5 | **Meyer v. Bremen.** The Messenger of Love } Compan- { | *r* | |
| 6 | — On the Way Home } ions. { | *r* | |
| 11 | — Saying the Prayer | *i r* | |
| 15 | — Blind Man's Buff | *i r* / | |
| 16 | — The Love Letter (Companion to No. 349) | *r* | |
| 32 | — The Declaration of Love | *r* | |
| 36 | — Expectation | *i r* / | |
| 42 | · Girl Knitting | *e* | |
| 43 | — Without a Home | *r* | |

2178.  MUNTHE—WINTER.

* The letters e n i r f indicate the sizes in which the photos are published.  For prices see p. 22.

| No. | ARTIST AND TITLE | Photographs Sizes.* | Gravures. Size. Price. |
|---|---|---|---|
| 46 | **Meyer, v. Bremen.** Secret Correspondence | r | |
| 49 | — The Portrait of Her Lover | r | |
| 60 | — The Toilet (Companion to No. 77) | i r | |
| 61 | — Fisher Woman ⎫ Companions | i r f | |
| 62 | — Shepherdess ⎭ | i r f | |
| 67 | — Rest of the Model | i r | |
| 71 | — A Little Joker ⎫ Companions | r | |
| 76 | — Luncheon ⎭ | r | |
| 77 | — Birthday Morning (Companion to No. 60) | i r | |
| 80 | — In the Twilight ⎫ Companions | r | |
| 81 | — Before the Bath ⎭ | r | |
| 82 | — Thoughtful | r | |
| 113 | — The Sick Pet | r | |
| 153 | — At the Fountain ⎫ Companions | i r f | |
| 163 | — Bo-peep ⎭ | i r f | |
| 183 | — Jealous | i r | |
| 205 | — Say Yes, Mother ⎫ Companions | i r | |
| 206 | — He Comes ⎭ | i r | |
| 219 | — Come Back | i | |
| 220 | — Leisure Hour | i | |
| 221 | — The Beginning ⎫ Companions | i r | |
| 233 | — Tired Out ⎭ | i r | |
| 245 | — The Prayer | i r | |
| 246 | — At the Cradle ⎫ Companions | i r | |
| 286 | — Mother's Care ⎭ | i r | |
| 282 | — Domestic Industry (Companion to No. 357) | i r | |
| 347 | — Yes or No? | i r | |
| 349 | — Morning Dream (Companion to No. 16) | i r f | |
| 357 | — First Say Your Prayer (Companion to No. 282) | i r | |
| 430 | — The Widow's Prayer | i r | |
| 432 | — Flower Girl | r | |
| 438 | — Tired of Learning | r | |
| 573 | — Messenger of Love | i r | |
| 635 | — Resignation | r | |
| 657 | — The Children's Pet | i r | |
| 661 | — First a Kiss! (Companion to No. 1221) | i r f | |
| 672 | — What Has Mother Brought Home? ⎫ Companions | i r f | |
| 691 | — In Which Hand? ⎭ | i r | |
| 700 | — Disappointed | i r | |
| 701 | — A Difficult Sum | r | |
| 702 | — A Penny a Bunch, Sir! (Companion to No. 767) | r | |
| 703 | — For Mother's Fire | r | |
| 764 | — Confidential Communication | i r | |
| 765 | — Little House-wife | i r | |
| 766 | — The First at the Well | r | |
| 767 | — Ruddier than a Cherry (Companion to No. 702) | r | |
| 785 | — Who 'll Buy a Rabbit? | i r | |
| 786 | — Village Gossip | i r | |
| 835 | — The Little Baby (Companion to No. 867) | i r | |
| 836 | — Little Wood Brook | r | |
| 837 | — A Love Tale | r | |
| 867 | — Come to Me, Darling! (Companion to No. 835) | i r | |
| 973 | — Going to School | i r | |
| 1141 | — Good Morning, Papa! | f | |
| 1184 | — The Dangerous Path | f | |
| 1221 | — The Study in Danger (Companion to No. 661) | i f | |
| 1222 | — First a Kiss! ⎫ Companions | i f | 17x12 $5 |
| 1249 | — Hush, Baby Brother's Asleep ⎭ | i f | 17x12 5 |
| 1442 | — Reading a Love Letter | i f | |
| 1458 | — At the Well | i f | |
| 1518 | — Birthday Morning | i f | |
| 1581 | — Who Is It? | i f | |
| 1590 | — The Little Thief | i f | |

* The letters e a i r f indicate the sizes in which the photos are published. For prices see p. xx.

| N. | ARTIST AND TITLE. | Photographs Sizes.* | Gravures Size. Price. |
|---|---|---|---|
| 1639 | **Meyer, v. Bremen.** Our Darling . . | i f | |
| 1692 | — Siesta ⎰ Companions . | i i f | 16½x12 $5 |
| 1693 | — The Wounded Lamb ⎱ | i i f | 16½x12 5 |
| 1727 | — Old Love Letters | . f | |
| 1728 | — At the Toilet . | . f | |
| 1729 | — The Little Rogue | f | |
| 1730 | — Girl Reading . | f | |
| 1731 | — Lessons for School . | f | |
| 1732 | — Obtaining Pardon . | f | |
| 1733 | — An Important Secret . | f | |
| 1745 | — Morning Toilet . | f | |
| 1746 | — Bad Notes From School | f | |
| 1747 | — Little Beggars . | f | |
| 1748 | — Birthday Preparations | f | |

Copyright, 1892, by Photographische Gesellschaft.

2219. NAUJOK – ST. CECILIA.

| 1749 | — At the Window . | f | |
| 1750 | — In Charge . | f | |
| 1755 | — Trust in God | | |
| | **Meyer von Bremen-Album.** (See Part VI.) | | |
| 1965 | **Meyer-Mainz, J.** Matinée . | | |
| 31 | **Meyerheim, Paul.** Menagerie in the Village | r | |
| 117 | — Young Savoyards Travelling | r | |
| 171 | — After the Hunt . | e i r | |
| 208 | — Sheep-shearing ⎰ Companions | e i r | |
| 209 | — Making Hay ⎱ | e i r | |
| 679 | — A Country Show | i r | |
| 680 | — Down the Hill . | i r | |
| 913 | — Lions . | e i f | |

* The letters e n i r f indicate the sizes in which the photos are published. For prices see p. xx.

| No. | ARTIST AND TITLE | Photographs Size * | Engravings Size | Price |
|---|---|---|---|---|
| 954 | **Meyerheim, Paul.** In the Palace Court (Companion to No. 958) | e f | | |
| 958 | — Roes | i f | | |
| 956 | — Black-game | i f | | |
| 957 | — Twelve-horned Stag | i f | | |
| 958 | — Small Game (Companion to No. 954) | i f | | |
| 1251 | — Emperor William I. | i | | |
| 1326 | — The Goat-dealer | | | |
| 1327 | — Village Street | i f | | |
| 1357 | — A Spring Night | i f | | |
| 1807 | — Chodowiecki | r f | | |
| 1849 | — Veronica | | | |
| 1776 | **Meyn, G.** Frederick the Great (Half length) | e i f | | |
| 52a | **Mieris.** The Studio of the Artist (Dresden) | i f | | |
| 174a | **Mignard.** Maria Mancini (Berlin) | e i f | | |
| 156a | **Milanese School** (formerly attributed to Correggio). The Handkerchief of Veronica (Berlin) | e i f | | |
| 2267 | **Millais, John.** The Vale of Rest (for Artist's Proofs, see Part I.) | | 17x25 | $12 |
| 2289 | **Millet, F. D.** A Love Letter | | 12x20½ | 5 |
| 1812 | **Mion, Luigi.** Early Morning ⎫ Companions | i f | | |
| 1813 | — After Mass ⎭ | i f | | |
| 2148 | **Molitor, F.** The Good Shepherd ⎫ Companions | i f | | |
| 2149 | — The Prodigal Son ⎭ | i f | | |
| 2232 | — Sacred Heart | i f | 20x12 | 5 |
| 2287 | — Sacred Heart of St. Mary | i f | 20x12 | 5 |
| 2041 | **Moore, H.** The Clearness after Rain | n i f | 20x29½ | 10 |
| 2120 | — Wrecked at the Harbor's Mouth | n i f | 18x29½ | 10 |
| 1826 | **Morgan, Fr.** A Heavy Load | i f | 21x14 | 5 |
| 1827 | — A Gentle Reminder | r f | 10x12 | 3 |
| 1906 | — The Tired Gleaners (Companion to No. 1326) | i f | 21x14 | 5 |
| 2146 | — Watching and Waiting | i f | 16x20 | 5 |
| 1308 | **Morten-Müller.** Norwegian Lake | i | | |
| 1796 | **Moscheles, F.** Would You Like It | r f | | |
| 576 | **Mücke, C.** Little Pepita | i r f | | |
| 1925 | — Amusing Baby | r f | | |
| 2402 | **Müller, A.** St. Cecilia | i f | | |

The FOLIO-EDITION of our photographs on India paper, with white margin, is especially adapted for portfolio-collections.

We have artistic PORTFOLIOS for this size at $4.00.

With an order for 25 or more photos, Folio size, they will be given free of charge.

2118.   SCHWENINGER—THE FIRST CLOUD.

* The letters e n i r f indicate the sizes in which the photos are published. For prices see p. 20.

*The edition of our photographs in small size as "BOUDOIR CARDS," on heavy black cardboard, with gilt bevelled edges, is frequently used for choice Christmas and New Year's cards.*

1795. SINKEL—CHRIST CHILD WITH IVTH COMMANDMENT.

| No. | ARTIST AND TITLE | Photographs No. | Sizes | Prices |
|---|---|---|---|---|
| 304 | **Müller, C.** Holy Family (Companion to Nos. 1589 and 1698) | c i r f | 16½x10½ | 85 |
| 351 | — The Holy Virgin | i r f | | |
| 783 | — Madonna of the Grotto | i r f | 19x13 | 5 |
| 1164 | — Immaculate Conception | c i r f | | |
| 1446 | — St. Anne with Infant Mary ⎫ Companions | i r f | 19x9 | 5 |
| 1447 | — St. Joseph with Infant Jesus ⎭ | r r f | 19x9 | 5 |
| | For facsimile gravures in colors of the two above see Part II | | | |
| 1589 | — The Holy Night (Companion to Nos. 304 and 1698) | c i r f | 16½x16½ | 5 |
| | *The original is in possession of the Berlin Photographic Company.* | | | |
| 1631 | — Immaculate Conception (Detail from No. 1164) | i f | | |
| 1698 | — Mary and Elizabeth (Companion to Nos. 304 and 1589) | c i r f | 16½x16½ | 5 |
| 1845 | — Christ and the Disciples in Emmaus | c i | | |
| 1846 | — St. Anthony of Padua and St. Gertrude ⎫ Com- | n i | | |
| 1847 | — St. Elizabeth of Thuringia and St. Vincent ⎬ panions | | | |
| | of Paula | n i | | |
| 1958 | **Müller, Fr.** Sacred Heart of Jesus | i | | |
| 2271 | — The Annunciation | i f | 19x14 | 5 |
| 2275 | — St. Mary | i f | 19x14 | 5 |
| 360 | **Müller, G.** Renunciation | i r f | | |
| 2227 | **Munier, E.** Cupid in Ambush | i f | 20x14½ | 5 |
| 2276 | — Bonjour, Petite Maman | i f | 20x15 | 5 |
| 2178 | **Munthe, L.** Winter | i f | 11x21 | |
| 26a | **Murillo.** Madonna (Dresden) | f | | |
| 27a | — St. Rodríguez (Dresden) | f | | |
| 109a | — The Birth of the Virgin (Paris) | r f | | |
| 113a | — Penitent Magdalen (Berlin) | i r f | | |
| 119a | — Immaculate Conception (Paris) | c i r f | | |
| 155a | — St. Anthony of Padua (Berlin) | c i f | | |
| 189a | — St. Anthony of Padua with Christ Child, part from above (Berlin) | i | | |
| 2219 | **Naujok, G.** St. Cecilia | n i | 20x15½ | 5 |
| 683 | **Neal, David.** Study head | i r | | |
| 778 | — Mary Stuart and Ricci | c i r f | | |
| 941 | — Study head | i | | |
| 1201 | — La Châtelaine (Study head) | i | | |
| 1336 | — Consolation | i | | |
| 1473 | — Oliver Cromwell Visiting John Milton | c i | 14½x18½ | 5 |
| 1925 | — Study head | f | | |
| 50a | **Netscher.** The Letter-writer (Dresden) | f | | |

\* *The letters c n i r f indicate the sizes in which the photos are published. For prices see p. 20.*

| N. | ARTIST AND TITLE. | Photographs Sizes.* | Gravures Size. Price. |
|---|---|---|---|
| 1451 | **Neuhaus, F.** King Frederick William I. Meeting a Troup of Emigrants from Salzburg | e i f | |
| 1580 | — The Great Elector at The Hague | i f | |
| 2163 | — Marshall "Vorwärts" | i f | |
| 2357 | **Neuhaus, H.** The Prodigal Son | i | |
| 2384 | — Poor Lazarus | r f | |
| 1478 | **Nicolet, G.** In the Palmgarden at Spaa | i f | |
| 1699 | **Niethe, E.** Corvette in a Calm | i f | 13x18 $5 |
| 2093 | **Nightingale, L. C.** A Foretaste of Summer ⎱ Com- | i f | 10½x20½ 5 |
| 2277 | — A Corner of the Lake ⎰ panions | i f | 10½x20½ 5 |
| 2402 | — Dawn of Summer (for Artist's Proofs, see Part I.) | | |
| 2193 | **Niss, Th.** Summer Night | i f | 19x16 5 |
| 94 | **Noack, A.** Religious Discussion at Marburg | i r | |
| 2027 | **Nonnenbruch, M.** Grecian Girl Bearing a Vase | i f | |
| 2155 | — Spring Blossoms | r f | |
| 2396 | — Christin im Gebet | i f | |
| 2400 | — Bach Idyl | i f | |
| 109 | **Nordenberg, B.** The Last Journey ⎱ Companions | i r | |
| 122 | — The First Journey ⎰ | i r | |
| 1623 | **Oeder, G.** A November Day | i f | |
| 1903 | **Oer, A. M. v.** The Annunciation ⎱ Companions | r f | |
| 1904 | — Birth of Christ ⎰ | r f | |
| 2360 | **Oppler, E.** Am Klavier | i f | |
| 2133 | **Outin, S.** Wasted Explanations | i f | |
| | *The original is in possession of the Berlin Photographic Company.* | | |
| 2138 | — Honeymoon (Detail from the above) | i f | |
| 2274 | **Pallik-Bela.** In Mother's Keeping | i f | 20x14 5 |
| 14a | **Palma Vecchio.** The Three Sisters (Dresden) | f | |
| 167a | — Female Portrait (Berlin) | i f | |
| 1332 | **Papperitz, G.** After Dinner | i f | |
| 1579 | — Mother's Happiness | i f | |
| 1673 | — Madonna | i f | |
| 1783 | — Adrian Brouwer and his Models | i f | 20x14 5 |
| 1836 | — Idyl | i f | |
| 1898 | — Hebe | i f | 20½x9 5 |
| 1939 | — Honeymoon (Companion to No. 1783) | i f | 20½x14 5 |
| 1988 | — Is He Thinking of Me? | i f | |
| 2004 | — Romeo and Juliet | e i f | 20½x14 5 |
| 2015 | — The Rising Star | e i f | |
| 2109 | — After the Bath | i f | |
| 2110 | — Queen of Heaven | i f | |
| 2210 | — Nymph with Cupid | i f | |
| 2288 | — Nymph | i f | |
| 2319 | — Fisherman and Nymph | i f | |
| 2334 | **Parker, Sybil C.** Salvator Mundi | i f | |
| 2335 | — The Good Shepherd | r f | |
| 1831 | **Parlaghi, Vilma.** Ludwig Kossuth | i f | |
| 1832 | — Ludwig Kossuth (Bust of the above) | i f | |
| 241 | **Passini, L.** A Reading from Petrarca at Chioggia | i r | |
| 408 | — A Girl from Chioggia | i r | |
| 445 | — Girls from Ampezzo | r | |
| 446 | — The Laundry-girl | r | |
| 447 | — The Needle-woman | r | |
| 448 | — In Church | r | |
| 449 | — A Magdalen | r | |
| 450 | — The Rescue | r | |
| 665 | — Procession in Venice | e i r | |
| 1302 | — In the Vestry | i f | |
| 1593 | — An Interesting Story | i f | |
| 1760 | **Paul, H.** Iphigenia | r f | |
| 252 | **Paulsen, Fr.** Mother's Pride ⎱ Companions | i r | |
| 457 | — A New Toy ⎰ | i r | |
| 1335 | — Servant's Employment Office | i f | |

*\* The letters e n i r f indicate the sizes in which the photos are published. For prices see p. 20.*

Our reproductions are the only ones
taken from the original of Richter's
"QUEEN LOUISE," in the Museum
of Cologne. They are published in the
following editions:

*FULL FIGURE.*
*HALF LENGTH (Oval).*
*BUST (Oval).*

For particulars see page 55.

1171. RICHTER—QUEEN LOUISE.

| | ARTIST AND TITLE | Photographs | Gravure Prints |
|---|---|---|---|
| 2028 | **Paulsen, Fr.** A Visit | *i* | |
| 2331 | **Pausinger, F. v.** A Stag | *i* | |
| 2357 | **Pauwels, F.** "So ihr mich von ganzem Herzen suchet" | *i* | |
| 2205 | **Perez, A.** La Toilette | | |
| 2365 | — En Excursion | | |
| 2366 | — L'Arrivée | | |
| 2367 | — La Rencontre | (See Facsimile gravures, Part II.) | |
| 2368 | — Au Jardin | | |
| 2007 | **Perrault, L.** Le Miroir Naturel | *i* | |
| 2217 | — Happy Sleep | *i* | |
| 2218 | — Diane | *r* | |
| 2087 | **Perrey, L.** Liseuse distraite | *r* | |
| 2060 | — Phoebe | Companions | *i* |
| 2145 | — Diana | | *i* |
| 2391 | — Stella | *i* | |
| 2310 | **Peske, G.** Good Friends | *i* | |
| 1618 | **Pfannschmidt, C. G.** The Adoration of the Magi | *i* | |
| 1619 | — The Star of Bethlehem | *i* | |
| 1641 | — The Annunciation | Companions | *i* | 18×13 | 8/- |
| 1642 | — The Adoration of the Shepherds | | *i* | 18×13 | 5 |
| 1647 | — The Resurrection | *u i* | |
| 1675 | — The Three Marias at the Tomb of Christ | Compan- | *i* |
| 1676 | — Angels Announcing the Resurrection of Christ | ions | *i* |

* The letters *n i r f* indicate the sizes in which the photos are published. For prices see p. 10.

| No. | ARTIST AND TITLE. | Photographs Sizes.* | Gravures. Size. Price. |
|---|---|---|---|
| 1709 | **Pfannschmidt, C. G.** The Burial of Christ } Companions | n i f | |
| 1710 | — The Women at the Grave of Christ } | n i f | |
| 1737 | — Poor Lazarus | r f | |
| 1738 | — The Rich Man Feasting } | r f | |
| 1739 | — Christ Mocked by the Soldiers } Companions | r f | |
| 1740 | — Crucifixion | r f | |
| 1741 | — Christ Enthroned | r f | |
| 1742 | — The Saviour Calling } | r f | 20x11  $5 |
| 1743 | — The Wise Virgins } Companions | r f | |
| 1744 | — The Foolish Virgins } | r f | |
| 1771 | — Madonna | r f | |
| 1772 | — Suffer Little Children to Come unto Me | r f | 14½x10  3 |
| 1793 | — David } Companions | i f | |
| 1794 | — Cecilia } | i f | |
| 495 | **Piloty, C. v.** Wallenstein on His Way to Eger | c i r f | |
| 1197 | — Girondists on Their Way to the Guillotine | c i r f | |
| 1352 | — The Wise and Foolish Virgins | c i r f | |
| 752 | **Plockhorst, B.** Emperor William I } Companions | c i r f | |
| 753 | — Empress Augusta } | c i r f | |
| 2397 | — The Good Samaritan | n i f | |
| 1284 | **Pohle, Leon.** Portrait of Ludwig Richter | f | |
| 1655 | — Thuringian Girl | f | |
| 2032 | **Pötzelberger, R.** Old Songs | i f | 12½x20  5 |
| 2033 | — Harmony | r f | |
| 2081 | — Tired of Waiting | i f | |
| 2330 | — Farewell | i f | 15x19  5 |
| 1770 | **Possin, R.** The Runaway | f | |
| 28a | **Poussin.** Venus Asleep (Dresden) | f | |
| 185a | — Roman Campagna (Berlin) | r f | |
| 1714 | **Poynter, Edw. J.** Diadumene (Before the Bath) | i f | 20x12  5 |
| 1789 | — A Corner in the Market-Place | i f | 14x14  5 |
| 2094 | — A Visit to Æsculapius | n i f | 19x29  12 |
| 1921 | **Prell, H.** Emperor William II. on Board of His Yacht Hohenzollern | c i f | |
| 1364 | **Preyer, P.** The Time of Roses | f | |
| 2222 | **Prinsep, V. C.** First Awakening of Eve | f | 16x19  5 |
| 2216 | **Prion, L.** Le Billet de Logement | f | |
| 2374 | **Puig-Roda, G.** Marchand d'Oranges | f | |
| 2401 | — Chez le Cordonier | f | |
| 720 | **Raab, G.** Elisabeth, Empress of Austria } | i r | |
| 721 | — Francis Joseph, Emperor of Austria } Companions | i r | |
| 722 | — Rudolph, late Crownprince of } (painted 1875) Austria | i r | |
| 1612 | **Rae, H.** Ariadne | i f | |
| 1866 | — A Naiad | i f | 21x14  5 |
| 2255 | — Spring Flowers | i f | |
| 1a | **Rafael.** Madonna di San Sisto | c i f | |
| 61a | — Madonna di San Sisto (Bust) } (Dresden) | n i f | |
| 65a | — Cupids of the Sistine Madonna } | n i f | |
|  | For editions from the original, see Part V. | | |
| 101a | — St. Michael (Paris) } Companions | n i r f | |
| 102a | — St. Marguerita (Paris) } | n i r f | |
| 103a | — "La Vierge au Sommeil" (Paris) | c i r f | |
| 104a | — Portrait of Young Man (Paris) | i r f | |
| 105a | — Princess of Arragonia (Paris) | r f | |
| 106a | — "La Belle Jardinière" (Paris) | r f | |
| 116a | — "Madonna Della Sedia" (Florence) | c i r f | 16x16  5 |
| 120a | — "Madonna del Cardellino" (Florence) | c i f | |
| 153a | — "Madonna Colonna" (Berlin) | c i f | |
| 154a | — "St. Cecilia" (Bologna) | c i f | |
| 164a | — "Fornarina" (Florence) | c i f | |
| 180a | — "Madonna Terranova" (Berlin) | f | |

* The letters c n i r f indicate the sizes in which the photos are published. For prices see p. xv.

| No. | ARTIST AND TITLE | Photographs Size. | Gravure Price. |
|---|---|---|---|

181a **Rafael.** "Madonna del Granduca" (Florence) . . . . *i  f*
         *The following belong to the "Cupid and Psyche cyclus" in the Villa Farnesina at Rome:*

89a — Venus Points Out Psyche to Cupid . . . . *f*
90a — Cupid Asking the Three Graces for Their Assistance . *f*
91a — Venus Relating Her Grievances to Juno and Ceres . *f*
92a — Venus on Her Way to Seek Assistance from Jupiter . *f*
93a — Venus Desiring the Destruction of Psyche . . . *f*
94a — Mercury Descending in Search of Psyche . . . *f*
95a — Cupids Conveying Psyche to Venus . . . . *f*
96a — Psyche Presenting Proserpine's Box to Venus . . *f*
97a — Jupiter Embracing Cupid and Promising Him Aid . *f*
98a — Mercury Conveying Psyche to Olympus . . . *f*
99a — Venus and Cupid before the Judgment Seat of Jupiter in Olympus . . . . . . . . *f*
100a — Feast of the Gods in Olympus at the Nuptial of Cupid and Psyche . . . . . . . .
         **Rafael's** "Cupid and Psyche" in portfolio, see Part VI.

175b **Rau, E.** Amused . . . . . . . .
194a **Raudnitz, A.** In Good Keeping . . . . *i  f*
195b — An Apt Pupil . . . . . . *r  f*
196b — In Bad Temper . . . . . . . *f*
138a **Rembrandt.** Samson Threatening His Father-in-Law for Withholding His Wife from Him (Berlin) . *f*
163a — Portrait of Himself (Berlin) . . . . . *i  f*
165a — Portrait of Himself (Berlin) . . . . . *i  f*

Copyright, 1894, by Photographische Gesellschaft.

2397. PLOCKHORST—THE GOOD SAMARITAN.

* The letters e n i r f indicate the sizes in which the photos are published.  For prices see p. 20.

| No. | ARTIST AND TITLE. | Photographs Series.* | Gravures. Size. | Price. |
|---|---|---|---|---|
| 172a | **Rembrandt.** Portrait of His Wife Saskia (Berlin) | c i | f | |
| 37a | — Bust of a Laughing Girl (Dresden) | | f | |
| 38a | — Rembrandt and His Wife (Dresden) | c i | f | |
| 39a | — Bust of a Man (Dresden) | | f | |
| 19a | **Guido Reni.** Venus and Cupid (Dresden) | n i | f | |
| 20a | — Ecce Homo (Dresden) | i | f | 16½x13 85 |
| 112a | — Ecce Homo (London) | i r | f | |
| 114a | — Mater Dolorosa (Berlin) | i r | f | |
| 117a | — Aurora (Rome) | c i r | f | |
| 137a | — Beatrice Cenci (Rome) | i | f | |
| | **Rethel, A.** Posthumous Works. See Part VI. | | | |
| 2025 | **Rettig, H.** Called to Her Calling | i | f | |
| 2026 | — Two Friends | | f | |

Copyright, 1893, Photographische Gesellschaft.

2258. FIRLE—HARMONY.

| No. | ARTIST AND TITLE. | | Photographs Series.* | Gravures. Size. | Price. |
|---|---|---|---|---|---|
| 118a | **Reynolds.** Angels' Heads (London) | | c i r | f | |
| 187a | — Samuel (London) | Companions | i | f | |
| 188a | — The Age of Innocence (London) | | i | f | |
| 23a | **Ribera.** St. Maria of Egypt (Dresden) | | i | f | |
| 1808 | **Ribustini, U.** Madonna of the Holy Rosary | | c i | f | |
| 1901 | — Portrait of Leo XIII. | | i | f | |
| 2371 | **Ricci, A.** L'Improvisateur Toscane à la Noce | | n i | f | |
| 25 | **Richter, G.** Egyptian Girl | Companions | n i r | f | 16½x11½ 5 |
| 26 | — Neapolitan Boy | | n i r | f | 16½x11½ 5 |
| 69 | — Odalisque | | n i r | f | |
| 158 | — Roman Girl | | i r | f | |
| 397 | — Nicolai Alexandrowitsch, Grand Duke of Russia | | i r | f | |
| 406 | — Gipsy-Boy | | n i r | f | |
| 427 | — Building the Pyramids | | c i r | f | |
| 588 | — Mother's Happiness | Companions | c i r | f | |
| 589 | — Father's Joy | | c i r | f | |

* The letters c n i r f indicate the sizes in which the photos are published. For prices see p. xx.

| No. | Artist and Title | Photographs Sizes.* | Gravures Size. Price. |
|---|---|---|---|
| 612 | Richter, G. Gipsy Girl | e i r f | |
| 545 | — The Two Brothers | n i r f | |
| 693 | — Gipsy Girl | i r f | |
| 725 | — Maria Paulowna, Grand Duchess Wladimir of Russia | e i r | |
| 730 | — Oriental Lady | r | |
| 731 | — Dusting the Pictures | r | |
| 776 | — Revery (Companion No. 1419) | i r f | |
| 856 | — Jairus' Daughter | e i r f | |
| 901 | — Emperor William I. (Cuirassier Uniform, full length) | e i r f | |
| 914 | — Riding the Lion | i r f | |
| 1053 | — Emperor William I., (Bust) | i f | 18x15 $5 |
| 1075 | — Portrait of a Boy | i f | |
| 1076 | — Portrait of Countess K. | i f | |
| 1129 | — Empress Augusta | i | |
| 1171 | — Queen Louise | e i f | 34x21 15 |
| 1243 | — Portrait | e i f | |
| 1257 | — Gipsy Girl from Tauria | i f | |
| 1419 | — Far Away (Companion to No. 776) | i f | |
| 1519 | — Portrait of Himself | i f | |
| 1561 | — Study-Head for Queen Louise | i f | |
| 1646 | — Queen Louise (Bust) | i | |
| 1864 | — Queen Louise (half length) | e | |
| | Richter-Album. See Part VI. | | |
| 548 | Richter, H. Piccolo ) Companions | } r | |
| 549 | — Piccola | r | |
| 269 | Riefstahl, W. The Pantheon of Agrippa | e i | |
| 922 | — Forum Romanum | e i f | |
| 1657 | Riepenhausen, J. Madonna | f | |
| 1912 | Riley, Th. By Brink of Cooling Stream | r | 8x16½ 3 |
| 1713 | Ring, M. Water-Witch | r | |
| 2262 | — Revery | r | |
| 1810 | da Rios, L. Father's Not Coming | r | |
| 2351 | Rödig, ⁎. Beethoven (full figure) | f | |
| 2352 | — Beethoven (Bust) | i f | |
| 2411 | — Mozart (Full figure) | i f | |
| 2412 | — Mozart (Bust) | i f | |
| 2209 | Roeber, F. The Holy Night | f | 21x15 5 |
| 2394 | v. Roessler, A. Reveille | f | |
| 2a | Giulio Romano. "Madonna Della Catina" (Dresden) | | |
| 1780 | Rosen, G. v. Nordenskjöld | e i f | |
| 664 | Rosenthal, Toby E. Elaine | r f | |
| 671 | — Alone Excluded from Spring! (From Poem by Lenau) | r f | |
| 740 | — Morning Prayers at Sebastian Bach's | e i r f | 23x34 15 |
| 902 | — The Alarmed Boarding-School | e i r f | |
| 1098 | — Forbidden Longings | f | |
| 1316 | — Mother's Darling (From poem by Immermann) | i f | |
| 1426 | — A Vacant Place | i f | |
| 2179 | Roskovics, J. Hungarian Peasant Woman | i f | |
| 22a | Rotari. St. Magdalen (Dresden) | f | |
| 64a | Rotermund. The Entombment (Dresden) | e i f | |
| 2376 | Roth, A. Pietà | r f | |
| 1439 | Rotta, A. Niente da Fare | i f | |
| 1501 | — Il Grillo ) Companions | } i f | |
| 1502 | — Tentazioni di Micio ( | i f | |
| 1437 | Rotta, S. The First Prayer | f | |
| 1438 | — Les Amoureaux | f | |
| 1514 | — The Story Book | i f | |
| 1563 | Roubaud, Fr. Lesghiens | r f | |
| 1723 | Roux, Jean. Vestal Virgin's Offering | i f | |
| 2055 | Royer, L. Telemachus on the Isle of Calypso | i f | |
| 31a | Rubens. The Judgment of Paris (Dresden) | i f | |
| 32a | — The Garden of Love (Dresden) | i f | |
| 33a | — Rubens' Sons (Dresden) | i f | |

* The letters e n i r f indicate the sizes in which the photos are published. For prices see p. xx.

| No. | ARTIST AND TITLE. | Photographs Sizes.* | Gravures. Size. Price. |
|---|---|---|---|
| 1530 | — The Raising of Lazarus (Berlin) | c i | f |
| 1593 | — Infant Christ and Infant St. John with Angels (Berlin) | c i | f |
| 173a | — St. Cecilia (Berlin) | i | f |
| 179a | — Portrait of a Child of Rubens (Berlin) | i | f |
| 1955 | Rudow, L. The Reigning Princes of Germany | c i | f |
| 1984 | — The Imperial Family | c i | f |
| 2169 | Rusiñol, S. A Bohemian | i | f |
| 48a | Ruysdael. The Hunt—Landscape (Dresden) | i | f |
| 2395 | Dendy-Sadler, W. Chorus (For Artist's Proofs, see Part I) | i | f |
| 1399 | Salentin, H. Art Lover ) Companions | i | f |
| 1405 | — The Young Shepherdess ( | i | f |
| 1931 | Saltzmann, C. Emperor William II. Arriving at Kronstadt | n i | f | 14½x29½ $10 |
| 2114 | Sant, R. A. Little Stella | i | f | 18x15 5 |
| 175a | Savoldo. Venetian Lady (Berlin) | c i | f |
| 2022 | Scalbert, J. La Douche | r i | f |
| 1754 | Schaefer, M. In the Nursery | i | f |
| 1264 | Schauer, G. " It Is I, Mr. Bailiff " (from " William Tell ") | i | f |
| 1363 | — Brigand's Wife on the Flight | i | f |
| 1852 | Schennis, Fr. v. Park of Versailles | i | f |
| 859 | Scherres, C. Inundation (Companion to No. 1522) | i r | f |
| 1492 | — Hut in the Woods After a Thunderstorm | i | f |
| 1493 | — Winter Landscape | i | f |
| 1504 | — Landscape on the Havel | i | f |
| 1522 | — Landscape in April (Companion to No. 859) | i | f |
| 1493 | Scheurenberg, J. The Lord's Day | i | f |
| 1087 | Schloesser, H. Pandora Before Prometheus and Epimetheus | i | f |
| 1421 | Schmaedel, M. v. Vanity | i | f |
| 155 | Schmidt, Max. Solitude (Companion to No. 1559) | i r | f |
| 1452 | — Hut on the Lake (Companion to No. 1648) | i | f | 13x18 5 |
| 1510 | — Polyphemus ) | i | f |
| 1511 | — Nausikaa | Companions (Landscapes from the | i | f |
| 1512 | — Calypso | Odyssee) | i | f |
| 1513 | — Eumaeos | i | f |
| 1559 | — Forest (Companion to No. 155) | i | f |
| 1568 | — The Game-keeper's Hut | i | f |
| 1648 | — Landscape with Lake (Companion to No. 1452) | i | f | 13x18 5 |
| 1649 | — At the Spring | i | f |
| 1650 | — On the Downs | i | f |
| 1761 | — Landscape with Castle ) Companions | i | f | 20x13 5 |
| 1762 | — Sea View ( | i | f | 20x13 5 |
| 2236 | Schmidt-Constant. A Question | i | f |
| 2306 | — Honeymoon | i | f |
| 1706 | Schmitzberger, J. A Good Bag | r | f |
| 781 | Schneider, H. Van Dyck Painting the Children of Charles I. | c i r | f |
| 874 | — An Encounter on the Sea | c i r | f |
| 1123 | Schobelt, P. Venus and Bellona | i | f |
| 1092 | Scholtz, J. Volunteers in 1813 before King Frederick William III. of Prussia in Breslau | c i | f |
| 1669 | — Herman and Dorothy (from Goethe's epic poem) | i | f |
| 696 | Schrader, J. Frederick I., Elector of Brandenburg, receiving the Oath of Allegiance from Berlin and Colln, 1415 | c i r | f |
| 734 | — Cromwell in Whitehall | c i r | f |
| 871 | — Young Noble Lady | i r | f |
| 2050 | Schrader, R. Racing Day in Charlottenburg | i | f |
| 2142 | — An Anxious Moment | i | f |
| 2143 | — Steeple Chase | i | f |
| 2001 | Schröder, A. An Explanation ) Companions | r | f |
| 2047 | — Parental Joy ( | r | f |
| 2198 | Schroedter, G. At the Well | i | f |
| 2231 | — Major and Minor ) Companions | i | f |
| 2257 | — Time of Roses ( | i | f |
| 2302 | — Young Love | i | f |

* The letters c n i r f indicate the sizes in which the photos are published. For prices see p. xx.

2046. LEU—SUNSET NEAR CAPRI.

| No. | ARTIST AND TITLE | Photographs Sizes.* | Gravures. Size. Price. |
|---|---|---|---|
| 2386 | **Schroedter, G.**  Forget Me Not | f | |
| 2370 | **de Schryver, L.**  L'arrivée du Transatlantique | i  f | |
| 2385 | —  Avenue du Bois (published as facsimile gravure see Part II.) | | |
| 539 | **Schuch, Werner.**  Hard Times | i r f | |
| 1013 | —  Escort of the Corpse of Gustavus Adolphus from Lützen to Wolgast | e i  f | |
| 1508 | **Schüler, Max.**  General-fieldmarshall von Manteuffel | i | |
| 2244 | **Schuller, C.**  Gardeuse d'oies | | 14x20½  8 |
| 2301 | **Schultheiss, K.**  The Bee Keeper | r  f | |
| 2348 | —  Old Heads and Young Hearts | i  f | |
| 1799 | **Schultze, C.**  Landscape with Mill (Eifel Mountains) | i  f | 14x21  5 |
| 2379 | **Schürman, F.**  Pheasant Shooting | f | |
| 2075 | **Schwabe, E.**  Old Christmas Joys | f | |
| 2158 | —  A Delegation of Workmen | i  f | |
| 1996 | **Schweninger, C.**  Tête-à-Tête | f | |
| 1997 | —  Poetry | i  f | |
| 1998 | —  Reminiscences | i  f | |
| 2058 | —  The Garden of Love | f | |
| 2059 | —  Hildegard | f | |
| 2118 | —  The First Cloud } Companions | r  f | |
| 2150 | —  Evening } | r  f | |
| 1597 | **Schwenzen, H.**  A Flower of the Heath | f | |
| 1886 | —  The Little Truant | r  f | |
| 2159 | **Schwiering, H.**  A Children's Party | f | |
| 1977 | **Seifert, A.**  Hypatia | i  f | |
| 2315 | —  A Vow | i  f | |
| 2377 | **Seitz, O.**  A Wave | i  f | |
| 801 | **Sell, Chr.**  Battle of Königgratz | i r f | |
| 1259 | —Laying the Cable Between Berlin and Cologne | i  f | |

* The letters e n i r f indicate the sizes in which the photos are published.  For prices see p. 20.

| No. | ARTIST AND TITLE. | Photographs Sizes.* | Gravures. Sizes Price. |
|---|---|---|---|
| 1456 | **Sellmer, C.** The Poacher's Revenge . | f | |
| 1113 | **Sichel, N.** Girl from Thebe . | i | f |
| 1114 | — Little Johnnie . | | f |
| 1146 | — Fellah-girl (Companion to No. 1113) . | i | f |
| 1229 | — Grecian Girl . | i | f |
| 1299 | — Water Carrier ) | ) i | f |
| 1315 | — Sicilian Flower-Girl } Companions . | ) i | f |
| 1386 | — Pompeian Girl ) | i | f |
| 1401 | — Little Fritz . | | f |
| 1404 | — Cetheris (Companion to No. 1410) . | i | f |
| 1406 | — In Distress . | | f |
| 1410 | — At the Sea-shore (Companion to No. 1404) | i | f |
| 1414 | — Cleopatra . | i | f |
| 1449 | — Dalmatian Girl . | i | f |
| 1477 | — A Duo . | i | f |
| 1521 | — Deborah } Companions | ) i | f |
| 1522 | — Girl of Trastevere } | ) i | f |
| 1532 | — Alceste } Companions | ) i | f |
| 1544 | — The Favorite } | ) i | f |
| 1656 | — A Messenger of Love . | i | f |
| 1666 | — Egyptian Girl (Companion to No. 1853) | i | f |
| 1716 | — Gipsy Queen } Companions | ) i | f |
| 1717 | — Bajadere } | ) i | f |
| 1718 | — A Beauty of the Harem . | i | f |
| 1719 | — Egyptian Princess . | i | f |
| 1724 | — Summer . | | f |
| 1725 | — Odalisque . | | f |
| 1802 | — Aspasia . | | f |
| 1833 | — Yum-Yum . | e i | f |
| 1842 | — Mignon . | | f |
| 1853 | — Fatme (Companion to No. 1666) . | i | f |
| 1854 | — Fellahwife with Child . | i | f |
| 1910 | — In Bondage } Companions | ) i | f |
| 1911 | — Jephtha } | ) i | f |
| 1915 | — Neapolitan Girl . | i | f |
| 1916 | — A Roman Girl . | | f |
| 1917 | — Pascuccia . | | f |
| 2009 | — Judith . | i | f |
| 2017 | — Lydia . | r | f |
| 2035 | — Turandot . | | f |
| 2048 | — Vestal Virgin . | i | f |
| 2363 | — The Girls of Tanger . | i | f |
| 2364 | — Montenegrinian . | i | f |
| 1142 | **Siemiradzki, H. de.** The Living Torches of Nero | e i | f |
| 1176 | — The Sword Dance . | i | f | 10x20 85 |
| 1206 | — The Beggar . | i | f |
| 1214 | — He and She . | i | f |
| 1359 | — The Rock of Tiberius at Capri . | i | f |
| 1403 | — A Priest of Isis . | | f |
| 1520 | — Cremation of A South Russian Chief (Tenth century) . | c | |
| 1564 | — Summer Night in Old Pompeii . | i | f |
| 1567 | — Warriors of Swiatoslaw at a Ritual Massacre . | i | |
| 1594 | — The Song of the Slave . | i | f | 18x11 5 |
| 1651 | — Rural Scene . | | f |
| 1652 | — At the Fountain . | | f |
| 1797 | — Follow a Good Example . | i | f |
| 1803 | — Follow a Good Example (detail from the above) . | i | f |
| 1957 | — Phryne at Eleusis . | e i | f | 18x35 12 |
| 2073 | — Woman or Vase? . | e i | f | 21x29 12 |
| 2233 | — Representation Mimique du Jugement de Paris . | u i | f | 13x29 10 |
| 2087 | **Siepen, A.** "Good Luck" . | i | f |
| 562 | **Sinkel, H. J.** The Nativity . | r | f |

* The letters e i r f indicate the sizes in which the photos are published. For prices see p. 20.

1860. ITTENBACH—HOLY FAMILY.

* The letters c n i r f indicate the sizes in which the photos are published. For prices see p. 70.

The number of sacred subjects published by us is very large.

Among them are works by artists of the famous Düsseldorf School, such as DEGER, IT-TENBACH, CARL MÜL-LER, etc., who are represented in our collection by their best productions.

| No. | ARTIST AND TITLE. | Photographs Sizes.* | Gravures. Sizes. Price. |
|---|---|---|---|
| 580 | **Spangenberg, G.** Luther's Arrival at Worms | e i r | |
| 838 | — The Procession of Death | e i r f | |
| 1052 | — The Path of Virtue or of Vice | i f | |
| 1152 | — Will o' the Wisp | i f | |
| 1230 | — The Three Maries at the Holy Sepulchre | i f | |
| 1707 | — Young Luther at Mrs. Cotta's House | e i f | 15x21   $5 |
| 1708 | — St. John's Eve at Cologne | i f | |
| 2345 | **Speier, Chr.** A Cavalry Song | i f | |
| 924 | **Sperling, H.** He Comes | i f | |
| 2188 | — Taste ⎫ | i f | |
| 2189 | — Hearing ⎪        Companions | i f | |
| 2190 | — Scent ⎬ " The five Senses " in scenes from the | i f | |
| 2191 | — Feeling ⎪        life of dogs | i f | |
| 2192 | — Sight ⎭ | i f | |
| | — *The above together* as Paravent (Screen), folio-size, $5.00 | | |
| | — *The same,* as Photogravure in extra size | e | 15x34   12 |
| | *The originals are in possession of the Berlin Photographic Company* | | |
| 2246 | — Visit of Condolence | i f | |
| 2247 | — Reveries | i f | |
| 2311 | — Saved | i f | |
| 2097 | **Spielter, C.** Hard Times | f | |
| 2141 | — The Miniature | f | |
| 14 | **Steffeck, C.** Steeplechase (Companion to No. 633) | e i r f | |
| 24 | — Emperor William (Bust with helmet) | i | |
| 159 | — On Horseback | r | |
| 633 | — Hallali (Companion to No. 14) | i r | |
| 634 | — Visiting the Ill Friend | r | |
| 635 | — The Dead Foal | r | |
| 642 | — The Victor | e i r f | |
| 769 | — Before the Race | r f | |
| 779 | — The Victor of Weissenburg and Wörth | e i r f | |
| 807 | — Albrecht Achill in Fight with the Nuremberghers | i r f | |
| 832 | — Dogs at Play | i r f | |
| 845 | — A Gipsies' Rest | r | |
| 846 | — Good Hope from Buccaneer and Gosse | r | |
| 898 | — Mare and Young | r f | |
| 899 | — Boy and Hound | i r f | |
| 943 | — The Quitzows Marauding | i f | |
| 944 | — Emperor William | i f | |
| 945 | — Insurgent (Portrait of a horse) | f | |
| 946 | — Diedenhofen (Portrait of a horse) | f | |
| 993 | — General-Fieldmarshall v. Manteuffel | i f | |
| 994 | — Mare | f | |
| 1036 | — Pug-dog | f | |
| 1056 | — Gipsy-boys on Horseback | i f | |
| 1088 | — Stallions | f | |
| 1109 | — Vitus from Blue Gown and Perfection | f | |
| 1150 | — Linton (Portrait of a horse) | f | |
| 1151 | — A Rest at the Well | f | |
| 1186 | — Stolz from Rustic and Sweet Home | f | |
| 1247 | — Portrait of a horse | f | |
| 1253 | — Verveville (Portrait of a horse) | f | |
| 1254 | — Plappeville (Portrait of a horse) | f | |
| 1328 | — Portrait of a horse | f | |
| 1361 | — The First Victory | i f | |
| 1380 | — Portrait of a horse | f | |
| 1432 | — Mare with Foals | f | |
| 1465 | — Roes Pursued | i f | |
| 1466 | — Portrait of a boy | f | |
| 1682 | — Queen Louise and Her Two Eldest Sons | e i f | 19x14   5 |
| 1930 | **Steinmetz, Fr.** Souvenir of the 9th of March, 1888 | r f | |
| 2196 | **Stephens.** Summer | n i f | 15x29   12 |
| 2398 | **Stewart, J.** A Baptism (for Artist's Proofs, see Part I.) | | |

*\* The letters e n i r f indicate the sizes in which the photos are published. For prices see p. 20.*

| No. | ARTIST AND TITLE. | Photographs No. * | Gravures No. Price. |
|---|---|---|---|
| 1773 | **Stocks, M.** Hostile Brothers | f | |
| 1774 | — Pussy at Home | f | |
| 1775 | — The Evict | f | |
| 1863 | **Stone, Marcus.** In Love | c i f | 19x29 $12 |
| 1968 | — The Return | i f | 23x11 5 |
| 2220 | — Bright Summer | i f | 19x12 5 |
| 2151 | **Strudwick, J. M.** Elaine | i f | 21x15 5 |
| 2337 | **Strutt, Wm.** Watching for Stragglers | f | |
| 2338 | — A Cloud of Witnesses (for Artist's Proofs, see Part I.) | i f | |
| 1069 | **Stryowski, W.** Ruthenian Idyl | f | |
| 2167 | — A Summer Night on the Weichsel | i f | |

*The Berlin Photographic Co. has among its publications productions of the most diverging tendencies. To all art-lovers watching the development of modern art the portfolio containing the works of the Munich "SECESSIONISTS" will be of great interest.*

*For particulars see Part VI.*

2033   PÖTZELBERGER—HARMONY.

| No. | ARTIST AND TITLE. | Photographs | Gravures |
|---|---|---|---|
| 1536 | **Suykens, H.** Day of Confirmation | f | |
| 176a | **Teniers, d. J.** The Backgammon-Players (Berlin) | f | |
| 41a | **Terburg.** Lady Washing Her Hands (Dresden) | f | |
| 183a | — Paternal Instruction (Berlin) | f | |
| 684 | **Teschendorff, E.** Ariadne | r | |
| 2291 | **Thoma, H.** Spring Roundelay | | 13x10 3 |
| 2293 | — Landscape | | 10x13 3 |
| 2294 | — Ideal Summer Day | | 10x12 3 |
| 2123 | **Thumann, Paul.** Art Wins a Heart (Published also as facsimile gravure, see Part II.) | n i f | 20x15 5 |
| | *The original is in possession of the Berlin Photographic Company* | | |
| 515 | **Tidemand, A.** The Bridal Procession | c i r | |
| 643 | — Past and Future ⎱ Companions | i r | |
| 655 | — Family Prayers ⎰ | i r | |
| 737 | — Grandfather's Benediction | c i r | |

\* *The letters e u i r f indicate the sizes in which the photos are published. For prices see p. 10.*

| No. | ARTIST AND TITLE. | Photographs Sizes.* | Gravures. Size. Price. |
|---|---|---|---|
| 777 | **Tidemand & Morten-Müller.** Colonel Sinclair Landing at Romsdalen, 1612 | e i r | |
| 1599 | **Tischbein, d. A.** Portrait of Lessing when a Youth | | |
| 11a | **Titian.** The Tribute Money (Dresden) | i | |
| 12a | — Madonna and Woman in White (Dresden) | | |
| 13a | — Reposing Venus (Dresden) | n i | |
| 67a | — Girl with Vase (Dresden) | i | |
| 107a | — Titian's Mistress (Paris) | r | |
| 115a | — Lavinia (Berlin) | e i r | |
| 133a | — Portrait of a Daughter of Rob. Strozzi (Berlin) | | |
| 151a | — Head of Sleeping Venus (Dresden) | i | |
| 160a | — Flora (Florence) | e i | |
| 165a | — "La Bella di Tiziano" (Florence) | e i | |
| 177a | — Portrait of Himself (Berlin) | i | |
| 1621 | **Tobias, A.** The Little House-keeper | | |
| 2261 | **Torna, O.** On the Malar-see | | 20x15 $5 |
| 880 | **Treidler, Ad.** Charles V. and Francis I. | e i r | |
| 1562 | — At Ischia | i | |
| 1773 | — Maruccia (Italian Girl) | | |
| 1779 | — Roman Girl | | |
| 1869 | — Carneval in Rome | r | |
| 2106 | — Limoni | | |
| 2061 | **Trood, H. W.** Breakfast | i | 14x21   5 |
| 2297 | **v. Uhde, F.** The Actor | i | |
| 65 | **Unknown Artist.** Portrait of the Countess Potocka | i r | 16½x13   5 |
| 21a | **Varotari.** Study Head (Dresden) | | |
| 141 | **Vautier, B.** The Anniversary Dinner | e i r | |
| 216 | — A Funeral in the Country | e i r | |
| 348 | — Dancing-room in a Suabian Village | e i r | |
| 353 | — At the Solicitor's | e i r | |
| 542 | — Bible Lesson | e i r | |
| 572 | — The Mother's Illness | e i r | |
| 649 | — In the Cloisters | e i r | |
| 676 | — Snubbed | i r | |
| 741 | — The Bride's Departure from Home | e i r | 26x32   15 |
| 795 | — First Dancing Lesson (Companion to No. 1071) | e i r | 13x19   5 |
| 860 | — The Toilet | i r | |
| 916 | — Going to the Magistrate (Companion to Nos. 741 and 1900) | e i r | 13x20   5 |
| 950 | — A Curious Occurrence | | |
| 963 | — Hypochonder | | |
| 1071 | — A Pause in the Dance (Companion to No. 795) | e i | |
| 1175 | — The Cousin (Companion to No. 1407) | i | 14x19   5 |
| 1320 | — In the Barber's Shop | i | |
| 1407 | — Playing Old Maiden (Companion to No. 1175) | e i | 14x19   5 |
| 1523 | — Without the Painter's Permission | i | |
| 1900 | — The Christening (Companion to Nos. 741 and 916) | e i | 13x20   5 |
| 1978 | — Much Ado About Nothing | r | |
| 1993 | — The Morning Bath | i | |
| 2214 | — Not embarrassed | r | |
| 2407 | — Calling on the Friend | i | |
| | **Vautier-Album.** See Part VI. | | |
| 24a | **Velazquez.** Portrait of a Man (Dresden) | | |
| 49a | **van de Velde.** Ice-Sport (Dresden) | | |
| 15a | **Veronese.** The Marriage at Cana (Dresden) } Companions { n i | | |
| 16a | — The Adoration of the Magi (Dresden) } { n i | | |
| 17a | — Christ on the Cross (Dresden) | | |
| 149a | — Christ bearing the Cross (Dresden) | n i | |
| 2056 | **Vinea, F.** The Fortune-teller } Companions | i i | 15x20   5 |
| 2108 | — A New Cavalier } | i i | 15x20   5 |
| 2280 | — Viens à mon aide, Amour | | 20x14   5 |
| 1472 | **Vogel, H.** Luther Preaching at the Wartburg | e i | |
| 1914 | **Voillemot, Ch.** Spring | r | |
| 1915 | — L'orangère (Bust of a woman) | i | |

*The letters e n i r f indicate the sizes in which the photos are published. For prices see p. 90.

* The letters r n i r f indicate the sizes in which the photos are published. For prices see p. 10.

| No. | ARTIST AND TITLE. | Photographs Sizes. * | | Gravures Size. Price. |
|---|---|---|---|---|
| 2355 | **Wilke, H.** Socrates taking Leave of his Pupils | | f | |
| 1365 | **Williams-Haynes, J.** The Miniature | | f | 10x14 $3 |
| 2359 | — No Thoroughfare. (For Artist's Proofs see Part I.) | | | |
| 1867 | **Wimmer, R.** Portrait of Emperor William II. (Bust.) | i | i | |
| 2211 | — Emperor Wilhelm II. on horseback | i | i | |
| 1105 | **Wislicenus, H.** Spring | | i | f |
| 1106 | — Summer | Companions | i | f |
| 1107 | — Autumn | | i | f |
| 1108 | — Winter | | i | f |
| 2245 | **Wolff, W.** Hedda | | i | f |
| 1286 | **Woltze, B.** Lovers | | | f |
| 46a | **Wouwerman.** Starting for the Hunt (Dresden) | | | f |
| 2285 | **Wunderlich, H.** Holy Handkerchief of St. Veronica | | | f |
| 528 | **Wünnenberg, C.** The First-born. | | r | |
| 2346 | — Wooing (for Artist's Proof, see Part I.) | i | i | 20¾x12½ 5 |
| 1870 | **Zaak, G.,** How Happy Could I Be with Either | | i | f |
| 2312 | **Zieger, H & Becker.** Evening Idyl | | i | f |
| 1506 | **Ziegler, Th., Dr.** Martin Luther (after Lucas Cranach) | | i | f |
| 1829 | **Zimmermann, C.,** Stag and Roes | | i | f |
| 1830 | — Stag in Spring | | i | f |
| 25a | **Zurbaran,** St. Coelestin (Dresden) | | | f |

* The letters c n i r f indicate the sizes in which the photos are published.  For prices see p. 20.

Copyright by Photographische Gesellschaft

2248. CALDERON—ORPHANS.

# IV.

## SYNOPSIS OF A SELECTION OF POPULAR PICTURES

ARRANGED ALPHABETICALLY ACCORDING TO THE TITLES, WITH SHORT
EXPLANATIONS OF SUBJECTS

This Part contains a selection of popular pictures from Part III.

It is arranged alphabetically, according to their titles, including a list of portraits of prominent persons, and is intended for the use of those not familiar with the names of the artists.

1172. GUIDO RENI—AURORA

# IV.

**Synopsis of a selection of popular pictures, arranged alphabetically, according to titles, with short explanations of subjects.**

Full particulars of the editions published of the pictures mentioned in the following list will be found in Part III., under the names of the respective artists.

| TITLE. | ARTIST. | NO. |
|---|---|---|
| ADAGIO | J. C. HERTERICH. | 1777 |

Ideal female figure floating on the clouds, lulling little Cupids to sleep by the music of her violin.

| AFTERNOON IN HYDE PARK | J. v. CHELMINSKI. | 1821 |

Sporting scene in Rotten Row.

| AFTER THE BATH | G. PAPPERITZ. | 2109 |

Female figure.

| AFTER WATERLOO | A. GOW. | 2119 |

Napoleon and his troops on the retreat after the battle of 1814

| AHASVER. (Original in the Metropolitan Museum of New York) | G. MARR. | 1217 |

| ALLEGRO | J. C. HERTERICH. | 1762 |

Ideal female figure arousing little Cupids from sleep.

| AMUSING STORY | ED. GRÜTZNER. | 1159 |

Jolly monks reading a humorous book.

| ARRIVAL AT SÄKKINGEN | R. ASSMUS. | 2215 |

Illustration to Scheffel's poem, "The Trumpeter of Säkkingen."

| ART WINS THE HEART | P. THUMANN. | 2123 |

Young Pompeiian painting a vase, while a young girl looks admiringly at his work. See illustration on page 35.

| THE ARTIST AND HER MODEL | L. KNAUS. | 1237 |

Woman artist painting little Cupid from life.

| TITLE. | ARTIST. | NO. |
|---|---|---|
| FAIRY OF THE ALPS | K. DIELITZ. | 1274 |

A chamois hunter sleeping near a rocky precipice while a mountain fairy guards his slumber.

| FAIRY TALE | G. GRAEF. | 1629 |
|---|---|---|

A raven is about to bear away the fish skin which a river nymph is casting off.

FALSTAFF SERIES:

| 1. FALSTAFF AND HIS PAGE | Ed. GRÜTZNER. | 891 |
|---|---|---|
| 2. "HERE I LAY AND THUS I BORE MY POINT" | " | 892 |
| 3. FALSTAFF IN BOAR'S HEAD TAVERN | " | 893 |
| 4. FALSTAFF ON THE BATTLE-FIELD | " | 894 |
| 5. FALSTAFF AND MRS. FORD | " | 895 |
| 6. FALSTAFF RECRUITING | " | 896 |
| 7. FALSTAFF AND BARDOLPH | " | 2223 |

| FARAGLIONI NEAR CAPRI | A. LEU. | 2045 |
|---|---|---|

| THE FAVORITE MARK | Ed. GRÜTZNER. | 628 |
|---|---|---|

| FELICIE | G. GRAEF. | 1163 |
|---|---|---|

Female figure.

| LA FIANCÉE | E. BISSON. | 2204 |
|---|---|---|

Female figure, half length, with Cupids.

| FIGHT BEHIND THE FENCE | L. KNAUS. | 2229 |
|---|---|---|

Boys settling a dispute.

| FIRE | K. DIELITZ. | 1528 |
|---|---|---|

Wotan's farewell to Brunhilde from "Walkure."

| FIRST CLOUD | C. SCHWENINGER. | 2118 |
|---|---|---|

Lovers in rococo costume; the young man is trying to reconcile his pouting sweetheart.
See illustration on page 46.

| FIRST LOVE | C. v. BODENHAUSEN. | 2040 |
|---|---|---|

Female figure, half-length.

| FLOREAL | E. BISSON. | 2238 |
|---|---|---|

Female figure with flowers.
See illustration on page 25.

| A FLOWER OF THE HEATH | H. SCHWENZEN. | 1597 |
|---|---|---|

Little girl standing in the heather.

| FORETASTE OF SUMMER | L. C. NIGHTINGALE. | 2093 |
|---|---|---|

Maiden sitting in a boat on the lake.

| FORTUNE TELLER | F. VINEA. | 2056 |
|---|---|---|

Scene in an Italian tavern in the XVIIth Century.

| GOETHE AND FRIEDERIKE | H. KAULBACH. | 1937 |
|---|---|---|

Goethe reciting his poems to Friederike.

| GOETHE IN SESENHEIM | A. BORCKMANN. | 561 |
|---|---|---|

The young poet introduced into the family of the parson.

| A GRECIAN SLAVE VASE-BEARER | H. NONNENBRUCH. | 2027 |
|---|---|---|

Female figure, half-length.

| GRETCHEN IN CHURCH | H. KAULBACH. | 1999 |
|---|---|---|

| HAPPY SLEEP | L. PERRAULT. | 2217 |
|---|---|---|

Cupid asleep.

| HARMONY | R. POETZELBERGER. | 2033 |
|---|---|---|

Young girl standing at the piano, with one hand gliding over the keyboard, lost in thought.
See illustration on page 59.

| HARMONY (A REHEARSAL) | W. FIRLE. | 2258 |
|---|---|---|

Young girls playing and singing to an old woman, who is listening attentively in an armchair.
See illustration on page 52.

QUEEN LOUISE OF PRUSSIA.  (See under Portraits)

A QUESTION . . . . . . . BLAIR LEIGHTON. 2224
  A young girl leaning against the garden wall while her lover in riding suit is standing before her.

RACING AT EPSOM DOWNS . . . . . . J. D. CULLIN. 2147

THE RAPE OF HELENA.  (Original in the Berlin National Gallery). R. V. DEUTSCH. 1122

READING FROM HOMER.  (Original in the Metropolitan Museum of New York) . . . . . . . . L. ALMA-TADEMA. 1672
  See illustration on page 23.

RECREATION.  (Single figure) . . . . . ED. GRÜTZNER. 853

ROMEO AND JULIET BEFORE FATHER LORENZO . C. BECKER. 1490

ROMEO AND JULIET . . . . G. PAPPERITZ. 2004
  The " Balcony Scene."

SACRED HEART . . . E. DEGER. 2089
  Christ, full figure, sitting.

SACRED HEART . . F. ITTENBACH. 879
  Full figure, standing.

SAPPHO AND ALKAEUS . . . L. ALMA-TADEMA 1342

SAVED . . . . . . . . . H. SPERLING. 2311
  A kitten protected by a large dog from the attacks of other dogs.
  See illustration on page 30.

THE SEASONS . . . . . . . WISLICENUS. 1105–8
  Series of four pictures representing allegorical female figures.

SÉRAPHINE . . . . . . . E. BISSON. 2237
  Female figure, half length.

Copyright, 1893, by Photographische Gesellschaft.

2277. NIGHTINGALE—A CORNER OF THE LAKE.

# V.

## REPRODUCTIONS FROM OLD MASTERS

### TAKEN FROM THE ORIGINALS IN EUROPEAN GALLERIES

This part contains the list of our reproductions from paintings in the following galleries:

*Berlin* (Royal Museum); *Brunswick* (Ducal Gallery); *Cassel* (Royal Gallery); *Dresden* (Royal Gallery); *Florence* (Pitti and Uffizi Galleries); *London* (National Gallery); *Paris* (Louvre).

While the larger part of them is published as *Photographs*, we have in recent years applied the *Gravure* process in our reproductions of ancient master-pieces, obtaining most excellent results. This has encouraged us to continue the publication of such standard works of the " old school" and we shall frequently make additions to our list of Gravures, which will thus eventually contain the foremost works of art in this novel and eminently perfected mode of reproduction.

## PHOTOGRAPHS.

The letters *e, n, i, r, f,* after each title, indicate the sizes, in which the same is published as photograph, viz.:

|  | Mounted. | Unmounted. |
|---|---|---|
| *e* = Extra size | $15 00 | $12 00 |
| *n* = Normal " | 10 00 | 8 00 |
| *i* = Imperial " | 4 00 | 3 00 |
| *r* = Royal " | 2 00 | 1 50 |
| *f* = Folio "  .  . | 75 | 60 |
| "  " per dozen | . | 6 00 |

A reduction of price, subject to a special agreement, will be made to purchasers of entire sets of single schools of art or galleries.

## GRAVURES.

" gr " means that the respective number is published as Gravure. The pictures of the Brunswick Gallery thus marked are published as *Gravures in folio size, printed on India paper* at the price of $1.50 each.

For the complete collection of the *Brunswick Gallery* in Portfolio and the *Rembrandts in the Cassel Gallery*, see Part VI.

For the Gravures of the *Sistine Madonna* and the *Holbein Madonna* see pp. 102 and 103.

47. FRA ANGELICO—THE LAST JUDGMENT.

# V.

# REPRODUCTIONS FROM OLD MASTERS.

* The letters e u i r f gr indicate the editions published of the respective picture. For prices see p. 76.

| | | | |
|---|---|---|---|
| 490 | **Aart van Antum.** Marine | Berlin | f |
| 632 | **Asselyn.** Battle of Lützen | Brunswick | f |
| 491 | **van Averkamp.** Landscape in Winter | Berlin | f |
| 693 | **Backer, Adr.** Rape of the Sabinians | Brunswick | f |
| 647 | **Bakhuizen.** Stormy Sea with Rocky Coast | Berlin | i |
| 648 | — A Light Breeze | " | i |
| 544 | **Bailleur the Elder.** The Adulteress before Christ | Brunswick | f |
| 177 | **Baldung, H.**, called **Grien.** Head of an Old Man | Berlin | f |
| 178 | — Crucifixion | " | f |
| 179 | — Altar (Centre, Adoration of the Magi; sides, St. Maurice and St. George) | " | f |
| 99 | **Fra Bartolommeo.** Madonna | Paris | i f |
| 100 | — The Descension from the Cross | Florence | f |
| 101 | — Assumption of the Virgin | Berlin | i |
| 269 | **Basaiti.** Madonna and Child | London | i |
| 584 | **van Bassen.** Interior of a Church | Berlin | i |
| 585 | — Interior of a Hall | " | i |
| 791 | **Battoni,** Penitent Magdalen | Dresden | e i f |
| 792 | — Achilles at the Court of Lycomedes | Florence | f |
| 670 | **Begeyn.** Landscape, Woods | Brunswick | f gr |
| 612 | **Beerstraaten.** Winter Landscape | Berlin | f |
| 669 | **Bellevois, J.** Sea Storm on a Rocky Coast | Brunswick | f gr |
| 153 | **Giovanni Bellini.** Dead Christ Supported by Two Angels | Berlin | i f |
| 154 | — Christ Mourned by Angels | " | i f |
| 155 | — Madonna and Child (School of Bellini) | " | f |
| 156 | — Leonardo Loredano | Dresden | i |
| 157 | — The Doge Leonardo Loredano | London | i |
| 158 | — Madonna and Child | " | i |
| 558 | **Bent, P.** Annunciation | Brunswick | f gr |
| 624 | **Berchem, Nic.** Winter Landscape | Berlin | i |
| 625 | — Landscape | Dresden | i |
| 626 | — Landscape with Cattle | " | r |
| 103 | **Bigio, Francia.** Portrait of a Young Man | Berlin | i |
| 104 | — Portrait of a Young Man | " | i |
| 105 | — David sees Bathsheba bathing | Dresden | i |
| 776 | **Biscaino.** The Nativity | Brunswick | f gr |
| 557 | **Bleker, D.** Bust of a Man | " | f gr |
| 671 | **Du Bois.** Landscape, Woods | " | f gr |
| 533 | **Bol, F.** Portrait of an Elderly Lady | Berlin | i |
| 534 | — Jacob's Dream | Dresden | c i |
| 535 | — Tobias and Sarah | Brunswick | f gr |
| 536 | — Male Portrait | " | f |
| 537 | — C. Duilius being Crowned with a Wreath of Laurel | " | f gr |
| 538 | — Pyrrhus and Fabritius | " | f gr |
| 306 | **Paris Bordone.** Madonna Enthroned, with Child and Saints | Berlin | e i f |
| 307 | — Female Portrait | London | i |
| 135 | **Borgognone.** Madonna Enthroned, with Child and Saints | Berlin | f |
| 136 | — Christ in the Garden of Gethsemane. Madonna Enthroned; Christ Bearing the Cross; 3 pieces | London | f |
| 67 | **Botticelli, Sandro.** The Virgin Mary Enthroned with Child and Angels | Berlin | i f |
| 68 | — Portrait of a Young Woman | " | f |
| 69 | — Portrait of Giuliano de Medici | " | f |
| 70 | — Madonna and Child Enthroned, and both St. Johns | " | f |
| 71 | — Venus | " | i f |
| 72 | — St. Sebastian | " | i f |
| 73 | — The Annunciation | " | i |
| 74 | — The Nativity | London | i |
| 75 | — Madonna and Child | " | i |
| 76 | — Madonna and Child | Paris | f |

* The letters e n i r f gr indicate the editions published of the respective picture. For prices see p. 76.

815. LANCRET—DANCERS.

* The letters e n l v f gr indicate the editions published of the respective picture. For prices see p. 76.

In ordering from this part it is well to bear in mind that all damages and cracks existing in the ancient paintings are faithfully reproduced in the photographs. We do not, however, reproduce paintings which have been too greatly injured to give an adequate idea of the original perfection.

730. MURILLO—YOUNG BEGGAR.

| | | | | |
|---|---|---|---|---|
| 793 | **Canaletto.** View of the Dogana di Mare and of the Church Sta. Maria della Salute, Venice | Berlin | i | f |
| 794 | — View of the Church Sta. Maria della Salute, Venice | | i | |
| 795 | — View of the Ducal Palace, the Piazetta and the Tower of St. Marcus | Berlin | i | |
| 796 | — View of Venice | Berlin | i | |
| 797 | — View of the Market Place at Pirna | Dresden | i | f |
| 798 | — View of the Church Sta. Maria della Salute | Paris | | f |
| 717 | **Cano.** St. Agnes | Berlin | i | f |
| 642 | **Van de Capelle.** Calm at Sea | | | f |
| 750 | **Caracci.** Head of Christ | Dresden | i | f |
| 751 | — Genius of Fame | | | r |
| 752 | — Shepherd and Shepherdess | Brunswick | | f |
| 753 | **Caravaggio.** Entombment | Berlin | e i | f |
| 754 | — St. Matthew | | e i | f |
| 755 | — Portrait of a Young Woman | | i | |
| 756 | — Cupid as Regent | | i | |
| 757 | — Cupid Vanquished | | i | |
| 758 | — Portrait of Himself | Brunswick | | |
| 144 | **Carpaccio.** Madonna and Child with Saints | Berlin | | f gr |
| 145 | — Confirmation of St. Stephen | | | f |
| 777 | **Castiglione.** Angels Appearing to the Shepherds | Brunswick | | f gr |
| 270 | **Catena.** Portrait of Count Raimund Fugger | Berlin | i | |
| 493 | **van Ceulen.** Bust of a Man | Brunswick | | f gr |
| 806 | **Champaigne.** Male Portrait | Florence | | |
| 780 | **Cignani.** Joseph and Potiphar's Wife | Dresden | i | f |
| 146 | **Cima da Conegliano.** Madonna Enthroned with Child and Saints | Berlin | | f |
| 147 | — Madonna and Child | | | f |
| 148 | — Christ | Dresden | e i | |
| 149 | — Head of Christ | | | r |
| 150 | — Presentation of Mary | Dresden | i | |
| 151 | — Madonna and Child | London | i | |
| 152 | — Madonna and Child, St. John and St. Magdalen | Paris | | |
| 808 | **Claude Lorrain.** Flight into Egypt | Dresden | i | f |
| 809 | — Coast of Sicily | | i | f |
| 810 | — Landscape | Berlin | i | f |

* The letters e n i r f gr indicate the editions published of the respective picture. For prices see p. 76.

*The harmony of the reproductions produced during recent years by the ISOCHROMATIC PROCESS makes them especially adapted for wall decorations, which even the uninitiated will not fail to appreciate. All the GRAV-URES published by us from the old Masters are based upon this process.*

559. FRANZ HALS—MALE PORTRAIT.

* *The letters e n i r f gr indicate the editions published of the respective picture. For prices see p. 76.*

| | | | | |
|---|---|---|---|---|
| 621 | **Cuyp, A.** Landscape | Berlin | | *f* |
| 622 | — Landscape with River | " | | *f* |
| 623 | — Boy with a Spaniel | Dresden | *i* | |
| 698 | **Cuyp, G.** Portrait of a Young Dutch Couple | Berlin | *i* | |
| 42 | **Gerard David.** The Crucifixion | Berlin | | *f* |
| 43 | — Canonicus with His Patron Saints | London | *i* | |
| 44 | **Style of Gerard David.** Christ at the Mount of Olives | Berlin | | *f* |
| 834 | **David, J. L.** Portrait of Mme. Récamier | Paris | | *f* |
| 835 | — Paris and Helena | " | | *f* |
| 580 | **Dirk van Delen.** Court of a Castle with People | Brunswick | | *f gr* |
| 839 | **Denner.** Portrait of an Old Man | Berlin | *i* | *f* |
| 840 | — Portrait of a Man | " | | *f* |
| 447 | **Diepenbeeck.** Marriage of St. Catherine | " | | *i* |
| 841 | **Dietrich.** The Waterfall at Tivoli | " | | *i* |
| 774 | **Dolci.** Jesus Christ | Dresden | *c i* | *f* |
| 775 | — St. Cecilia | " | *c i* | *f* |
| 767 | **Domenichino.** Portrait of the Architect Vincenzo Scamozzi | Berlin | *i* | *f* |
| 524 | **Dou, G.** Penitent Magdalen | " | | *f* |
| 525 | — Portrait of an Old Woman | " | | *f* |
| 526 | — The Hermit | Dresden | *i* | *f* |
| 527 | — Portrait of Himself | " | | *r* |
| 528 | — The Schoolmaster | " | *i* | *f* |
| 529 | — Violin Player | " | | *r* |
| 530 | — Dropsical Woman | Paris | | *f* |
| 531 | — Portrait of Himself | Brunswick | | *f gr* |
| 601 | **Droogsloot.** View of a Village Street | Dresden | *i* | |
| 451 | **Duchatel.** Portrait of a Young Flemish Nobleman | Berlin | *i* | *i* |
| 800 | **Dughet.** Roman Landscape | Dresden | *i* | |
| 167 | **Dürer.** Madonna | Berlin | | *f* |
| 168 | — Portrait of Jacob Muffel | " | *i* | *f* |
| 169 | — Bernhard of Ressen | Dresden | | *r* |
| 170 | — Christ on the Cross | " | | *f* |
| 171 | — Apostle St. Philipp | Florence | | *f* |
| 172 | — Apostle St. Jacob | " | | *f* |
| 173 | — Portrait of Himself | " | | *f* |
| 174 | — Portrait of a Senator | London | | *f* |
| 1670 | — Madonna with the Finch | Berlin | *i* | *f* |
| | (Purchased by the Old Museum in 1893.) | | | |
| | — *Complete collection of photographs from Engravings and Woodcuts in the Royal Museum at Berlin:* | | | |

Sundry Subjects, 34 folio photos, at 70c.; 12 cabinet photos at 35c.
Four Subjects from the Revelations of St. John. Folio photos at 70c.
Sixteen Subjects from the Small Passion from Dürer's Engravings. Cab. photos at 35c.

Life of the Virgin Mary:
Folio photos at . . . 70c.
Cabinet " " . . 35c.
The Large Passion:
Folio photos at . . 70c.
Cabinet " " . . 35c.
The Small Passion:
36 Cabinets at . . . 35c.
(From Dürer's original woodcuts.)

| | | | | |
|---|---|---|---|---|
| 630 | **Dujardin.** Evening | Berlin | | *f* |
| 631 | — Ox and Goats | Dresden | | *r* |
| 608 | **Dusart.** Peasants | Brunswick | | *f gr* |
| 412 | **van Dyck.** Portrait of Isabella, Daughter of Philipp II. | Berlin | *c i* | *f* |
| 413 | — Pietà | " | *c i* | *f* |
| 414 | — The Children of Charles I. of England | " | *c i* | *f* |
| 415 | — The Penitent Sinners | " | *c i* | *f* |
| 416 | — Portrait of Thomas François Carignan | " | *c i* | *f* |
| 417 | — Christ | " | *c* | *f* |
| 418 | — Portrait of a Man in Armor | Dresden | *i* | *f* |
| 419 | — Bust of a Man | " | *i* | *f* |
| 420 | — Danaë | " | *i* | *f* |
| 421 | — Henrietta Maria, Queen of England | " | *c i* | *f* |
| 422 | — Charles I., King of England | " | *c i* | *f* |
| 423 | — The Children of Charles I. | " | *c i* | *f* |
| 424 | — Mary, Queen of Heavens | " | *c i* | *f* |

*The letters c n i r f gr indicate the editions published of the respective picture. For prices see p. 76.*

414. VAN DYCK—THE CHILDREN OF CHARLES I.

| | | | | | | |
|---|---|---|---|---|---|---|
| 425 | **Van Dyck.** Portrait of a Man | Dresden | e | i | f | gr |
| 426 | — Male Portrait | " | | i | f | |
| 427 | — Portrait of a Man | " | | i | f | |
| 428 | — Rubens' Brother | " | | | f | |
| 429 | — Thomas Parr | | | i | f | |
| 430 | — Portrait of a Woman | " | e | i | f | gr |
| 431 | — Drunken Silen | " | | | f | |
| 432 | — Portrait of Cornelius van der Gest | London | | i | | |
| 433 | — Portrait of Himself | " | | i | | |
| 434 | — Portrait of Rubens | " | | i | | |
| 435 | — Madonna and Donors | Paris | | i | f | |
| 436 | — Portrait of a Man | " | | | f | |
| 437 | — Charles I. of England and Henriette of France | Florence | | | f | |
| 438 | — Repose on the Flight into Egypt | " | | | f | |
| 439 | — Portrait of a Man | Brunswick | | | f | gr |
| 4120 | — Family Portrait of Sebastian Leers with wife and child | Cassel | | i | | |
| 4121 | — Portrait of the Artist Snyders and his wife | " | | i | | |
| 4122 | — Female Portrait | " | | i | | |
| 539 | **v. d. Eeckhout.** Salomon Giving Offering to Foreign Gods | Brunswick | | | f | gr |
| 540 | — Mother and Child | " | | | f | gr |
| 541 | — Tobias Giving his Father Sight | " | | | f | gr |
| 542 | — Sophonisbe Receiving the Viol which Masinissa Sends to Her | " | | | f | |
| 836 | **Elsheimer.** Mountain Landscape with Ruins | " | | | f | gr |
| 718 | **Espinoso.** Christ Bearing the Cross | Dresden | | i | | |
| 488 | **Esselins.** Rocky Landscape with a Bathing Nymph | Brunswick | | | f | gr |
| 652 | **Everdingen.** Waterfall with Huts | " | | | f | gr |
| 653 | — Norwegian Highlands | " | | | f | gr |
| 1 | **Jan and Hubert van Eyck.** Singing Choir of Angels | Berlin | n | r | | |
| 2 | — Angels Playing Organ and Violin (St. Cecilia) | " | n | r | f | |
| 3 | — The Just Judges | " | n | r | f | |
| 4 | — The Soldiers of Christ | " | n | r | f | |
| 5 | — The Holy Anchorites | " | n | r | f | |
| 6 | — The Holy Pilgrims | " | n | r | f | |
| 7 | — Portrait of the Donor's Wife, Isabella Vyt | " | n | r | f | |
| 8 | — Portrait of the Donor, Jodocus Vyt | " | n | r | f | |

* The letters e n i r f gr indicate the editions published of the respective picture. For prices see p. 76.

*To those wishing to become more conversant with the history of ancient art, a visit to OUR GALLERY 14 EAST 23d STREET, (Madison Square, South), New York, will be found attractive and instructive, as the entire collections are constantly on view, arranged according to the different schools.*

1. VAN EYCK—SINGING ANGELS.

2. VAN EYCK—ANGELS PLAYING ORGAN, ETC.

| No. | | | | |
|---|---|---|---|---|
| 9 | **Jan and Hubert van Eyck.** The Virgin Mary | Berlin | n | f |
| 10 | — Gabriel (The Angel of the Annunciation) | | n | r f |
| 11 | — St. John, the Evangelist | " | n | r f |
| 12 | — St. John, the Baptist | " | n | r f |
| | (No. 1 to 12 from the altar of St. Bavo in Ghent). | | | |
| 13 | **Jan van Eyck.** Portrait of a Man with Pinks | " | i | |
| 14 | — Christ as King of Kings | " | i | |
| 15 | — The Virgin Mary with Child (Copy) | " | i | |
| 16 | — Altarpiece | Dresden | i | |
| 17 | — Annunciation (2 parts) | | | f |
| 18 | — Portrait of a Flemish Merchant and his Wife | London | i | |
| 19 | — Portrait of an Unknown Man | " | | r |
| 20 | — Portrait of a Man | " | | r |
| 21 | — Madonna | Paris | | r f |
| 543 | **Fabritius, B.** Peter in the House of Cornelius | Brunswick | | f gr |
| 108 | **Firenzo di Lorenzo.** Madonna and Child | Berlin | | f |
| 545 | **Flinck, G.** Female Portrait | Berlin | i | |
| 546 | — Young Girl in the Dress of a Shepherdess | " | | f gr |
| 338 | **Floris, Fr.** The Falcon Hunter | " | | f gr |
| 783 | **Franceschini.** Penitent Magdalen Surrounded by Women | Dresden | r i | |
| 124 | **Francia.** Virgin and Child | " | i | |
| 125 | — Holy Family | Berlin | i | |
| 126 | — Pieta | London | i | |
| 127 | — Christ on the Cross | Paris | i | f |
| 128 | **School of Francia.** Madonna and Child with St. John. | Berlin | i | |
| 351 | **Francken the Younger.** Neptune and Galatea | Brunswick | | f gr |
| 443 | **Fyt, J.** Diana with Her Game | Berlin | i | |
| 444 | — Two Horses | Brunswick | | f gr |
| 445 | — Birds | " | | f |
| 804 | **Gainsborough.** Portrait of Mrs. Siddons | London | r i | |
| 805 | — Portrait of Sir Bate Dudley | " | i | |
| 806 | — Orpin, Parish Clerk of Bradford | " | i | |
| 91 | **Raffaelino del Garbo.** Virgin with Child and Angels | Berlin | i | f |
| 92 | — The Virgin Mary and Child with Saints | " | i | f |
| 252 | **Garofalo.** Marriage of Bacchus and Ariadne | Dresden | i | |
| 253 | — Mars, Venus, and Cupid | " | i | |
| 254 | — Madonna Adoring the Child | " | r i | |

*The letters e n i r f gr indicate the editions published of the respective picture. For prices see p. 76.

725. MURILLO—MADONNA.

* The letters e n i r f gr indicate the editions published of the respective picture. For prices see p. 76.

| | | | | | |
|---|---|---|---|---|---|
| 573 | Dirk Hals. The Drinkers | Berlin | | | f |
| 559 | Franz Hals. Male Portrait | " | | i | f |
| 560 | — Female Portrait | " | | i | f |
| 561 | — Hille Bobbe, the Witch of Harlem | " | | i | f gr |
| 562 | — Portrait of Tymann Oosdorp | " | | i | f |
| 563 | — Portrait of a Young Man | " | | i | f |
| 564 | — Portrait of the Clergyman Joannes Acronius | " | | | f |
| 565 | — Portrait of a Nobleman | " | | | f |
| 566 | — Boy Singing | " | | i | |
| 567 | — Portrait of an Aged Man | " | | i | |
| 568 | — Nurse with Child | " | | i | |
| 569 | — The Jovial Trio (Copy) | " | | i | |
| 570 | — Male Portrait | Dresden | | | f |
| 571 | — Male Portrait | " | | | f |
| 572 | — Old Woman | " | | i | |
| 5590 | — The Singing Boys | Cassel | | i | |
| 333 | Heemskerk (Otto van Veen). Portrait of a Young Girl | Berlin | | | f |
| 334 | — Baptism of Christ | Brunswick | | | f |
| 574 | van der Helst. Portrait of an Old Woman | Berlin | | i | f |
| 575 | — Portrait of an Old Woman | " | | | f |
| 576 | — Male Portrait | Dresden | | i | |
| 577 | — Male Portrait | Florence | | | f |
| 578 | — Family Portrait | Brunswick | | | f gr |
| 628 | de Heusch. Rocky Italian Landscape | Brunswick | | | f gr |
| 673 | van der Heyden. Landscape with Old Castle and Bridge | " | | | f gr |
| 654 | Hobbema. Landscape with Woods | Berlin | | | f |
| 655 | — Landscape | Paris | | | f |
| 857 | Hogarth. The Marriage Contract | London | | i | |
| 858 | — After the Wedding | " | | i | |
| 859 | — At the Quack's | " | | i | |
| 860 | — In the Dressing Room of the Countess | " | | i | |
| 861 | — The Duel and Death of the Earl | " | | i | |
| 862 | — The Death of the Countess | " | | i | |
| 183 | Holbein the Younger. Portrait of a Man | Berlin | | i | f |
| 184 | — Portrait of a Young Man | " | | i | f |
| 185 | — Portrait of the Merchant George Gisze | " | e | i | f |
| 186 | — Portrait of a Young Man | " | | i | f |
| 187 | — Portrait of the Merchant Fallenn | Brunswick | | | f gr |
| 188 | — Madonna | Dresden | e | i | f |
| 189 | — Madonna (Bust) | " | | e | |
| 1830 | — Madonna of the Burgomaster Meyer (For particulars see page 32) | Darmstadt | | | gr |
| 190 | — Portrait of Hubert Morett | Dresden | e | i | f gr |
| 191 | — Sir Thomas and John Godsalue | " | | | r |
| 192 | — Portrait of an Old Man | Florence | | | f |
| 193 | — Portrait of Himself | " | | | f |
| 194 | — Portrait of a Lady | London | | i | |
| 707 | Hondekoeter. Cattle with the Ark of Noah in the Background | Brunswick | | | f |
| 494 | Honthorst. The Game of Backgammon | Berlin | | | f |
| 495 | — Boy with Flute | Brunswick | | | f gr |
| 353 | van Hulst. Flemish Fair | " | | | f gr |
| 713 | Huysum. Flowers | Dresden | | | r |
| 714 | — Flowers and Fruit | Florence | | | f |
| 715 | — Flowers in a Vase | Berlin | | i | |
| 716 | — Bouquet | " | | i | |
| 633 | de Jong, M. Gustavus Adolphus in the Battle of Lützen | Brunswick | | | f |
| 446 | Jordaens. The Beans Feast | " | | | f gr |
| 460 | — The Satyr at the Farmer's | Cassel | | i | |
| 461 | — Family Portrait | " | | i | |
| 843 | Angelika Kauffmann. Portrait of Herself | Berlin | | i | f |
| 844 | — Vestal Virgin | Dresden | e | i | f |

* The letters e n i r f gr indicate the editions published of the respective picture. For prices see p. 76.

831. MME. LE BRUN—PORTRAIT OF HERSELF AND HER DAUGHTER.

* The letters *e n i v f gr* indicate the editions published of the respective picture. For prices see p. 76.

837. SEIBOLD—MALE PORTRAIT.

| | | | | |
|---|---|---|---|---|
| 132 | **Lionardo da Vinci.** Portrait of Joconda (Mona Lisa) | Paris | | *f* |
| 133 | — La Monaca | Florence | | *f* |
| 133 | **School of Lionardo.** Christ and the Scribes | London | *i* | |
| 845 | **Liotard.** The Vienna Chocolate Girl | Dresden | *i* | *f* |
| 849 | — Mademoiselle Laverge | " | | |
| 61 | **Fra Filippo Lippi.** Madonna and Child | Berlin | | *f* |
| 62 | — Madonna Adoring the Child | " | *i* | *f* |
| 63 | — The Virgin Mary as Mother of Mercy | Berlin | | *f* |
| 64 | — John the Baptist and Six Saints | London | *i* | |
| 65 | — The Annunciation | " | | *r* |
| 66 | — Madonna | Florence | | *f* |
| 79 | **Filippino Lippi.** Portrait of a Young Man | Berlin | | *f* |
| 583 | **van Loo.** Rest During the Hunt | Paris | | *f* |
| 297 | **Lorenzo Lotto.** Portrait of Himself | Berlin | | *f* |
| 138 | **Luini.** Holy Family | Paris | | *f* |
| 472 | **Luykx.** Dead Game | Brunswick | | *f* *s* |
| 485 | **van der Lys.** Landscape with Bathing Nymphs | " | | *f* |
| 327 | **Mabuse (Jan Gossaert).** Madonna with Child | Berlin | | *f* |
| 328 | — Neptune and Amphitrite | " | | *f* |
| 329 | — Woman Weighing Gold | " | | *f* |
| 330 | — Portrait of a Man | London | *i* | |
| 555 | **Maes.** Portrait of the Baron Godard of Reede | Dresden | *i* | |
| 556 | — A Learned Man | Brunswick | | *f* *s* |
| 120 | **Mantegna.** Madonna and Child | Berlin | | *f* |
| 121 | — Portrait of a Clergyman | " | | *f* |
| 122 | — Presentation in the Temple | " | | *f* |
| 123 | — Madonna Enthroned, St. John, and Magdalen | London | *i* | |
| 778 | **Maratti.** Madonna and Child | Dresden | *i* | |
| 779 | — Virgin and Child | " | *i* | |
| 853 | **Maron.** Own Portrait | " | | *r* |
| 854 | — Julie Mengs | " | | *r* |
| 57 | **Masaccio.** Adoration of the Kings | Berlin | | *f* |
| 58 | — Martyrdom of St. Peter and St. John | " | | *f* |
| 59 | — Portrait of Himself | Florence | | *f* |
| 60 | — Portrait of an Old Man | " | | *f* |
| 321 | **Quinten Matsys.** Madonna Enthroned and Child | Berlin | *i* | *f* |
| 322 | — St. Jerome in His Cell | " | | *f* |
| 323 | — Portrait of a Young Man | " | | *f* |
| 324 | — The Saviour | London | | *r* |
| 325 | — Virgin Mary | " | *i* | |

* The letters o n i r f gr indicate the editions published of the respective picture. For prices see p. 76.

838. SEIBOLD—FEMALE PORTRAIT.

| | | | | |
|---|---|---|---|---|
| 675 | **van d. Meer v. Delft.** Lady with Necklace of Pearls. | Berlin | i | f |
| 676 | — Country House | " | | f |
| 677 | — Girl Reading. | Dresden | i | f |
| 678 | — Girl with Glass | Brunswick | | f gr |
| 665 | **van d. Meer v. Haarlem.** Dutch Marshy Landscape. | " | | f gr |
| 106 | **Melozzo da Forli.** Allegorical Representation of the Culture of Science at the Court of Urbino | Berlin | | f |
| 107 | — Another representation of the above | " | | f |
| 37 | **Hans Memling.** The Virgin Mary with the Child | " | i | f |
| 38 | — Anthony of Burgundy | Dresden | i | |
| 39 | — Madonna Enthroned | London | i | |
| 40 | — Madonna with Child | " | | r |
| 41 | — St. Lorenzo and St. John the Baptist | " | i | |
| 847 | **Raffael Mengs.** Cupid | Dresden | i | f |
| 848 | — Portrait of Himself (en face) | " | i | f |
| 849 | — Portrait of Himself (profile) | " | i | f |
| 850 | — Mengs' Father | " | i | f |
| 851 | — Mme. Thiele | " | i | |
| 852 | — Friedrich August the Just (child) | " | i | |
| 141 | **da Messina, A.** Madonna and Child | Berlin | i | f |
| 142 | — Portrait of a Young Man | " | i | f |
| 143 | — St. Sebastian | Dresden | | i f |
| 594 | **Metsu, G.** The Family of the Merchant Gelfing | Berlin | i | f |
| 595 | — The Cook | " | i | |
| 596 | — Portrait of a Woman | " | i | |
| 597 | **Metsu, G.** Girl Reading | Dresden | i | |
| 598 | — Lace Maker | " | | r f |
| 599 | — The Tavern | " | | r |
| 600 | — The Bar-maid | Brunswick | | f gr |
| 469 | **Meulener, P.** A Battle of the Duke Christian of Brunswick | " | | f gr |
| 243 | **Michel Angelo.** Madonna and Child | London | i | |
| 244 | — Entombment | " | | i |
| 245 | — Holy Family | Florence | | f |
| 476 | **Mierevelt.** Portrait of a Man | Dresden | | r |
| 477 | — Portrait of a Family | Brunswick | | f gr |
| 686 | **F. v. Mieris.** Studio of the Artist | Dresden | i | f |
| 687 | **W. v. Mieris.** Man in a Window Playing at the Trumpet | " | | r |
| 805 | **Mignard.** Portrait of Maria Mancini | Berlin | i | i f |

* The letters e n l r f gr indicate the editions published of the respective pictures. For prices see p. y.

| | | | |
|---|---|---|---|
| 712 | **Mignony.** Flowers in a Glass | Dresden | i |
| 268 | **School of Milan.** Handkerchief of Veronica | Berlin | i   j |
| 611 | **Molenaer.** Landscape with Women Washing | Brunswick | j |
| 616 | **Molyn the Elder.** Sandy Hill with Trees | " | j gr |
| 348 | **de Momper the Younger.** Summer | " | j gr |
| 335 | **Antony Mor.** Portrait of Cornelis van Horn and Antonis Taetz | Berlin | i   j |
| 336 | — Portrait of a Man | Dresden | r |
| 337 | — Man with Gloves | Brunswick | j gr |
| 552 | **Moyaert.** The Calling of Matthew | " | j gr |
| 473 | **Moreelse.** Portrait of a Man in Black | Dresden | i |
| 298 | **Moretto.** Mary and Elizabeth with Infant Christ and Infant John, Adored by Fra Bartolommeo Arnoldo | Berlin | n i   j |
| 299 | — Italian Nobleman | London | i |
| 300 | — Male Portrait | " | i |
| 301 | **Moroni.** Italian Nobleman | " | i |
| 302 | — Portrait of a Tailor | " | i |
| 303 | — Female Portrait | " | i |
| 304 | — Italian Clergyman | " | i |
| 305 | — Portrait of a Man of Letters | Berlin | i |
| 726 | **Murillo.** St. Anthony of Padua and the Infant Christ | " | e   i   j |
| 727 | — Female Portrait | " | n i   j |
| 728 | — Madonna | Dresden | e   i   j |
| 729 | — St. Rodrigues | " | i   j |
| 730 | — Spanish Peasant Boy | London | i |
| 731 | — Immaculate Conception | Paris | j |
| 732 | — Birth of the Virgin | " | i   j |
| 733 | — Madonna and Child | " | i   j |
| 734 | — Young Beggar | " | i   j |
| 735 | — St. Virgin and Child | Florence | j |
| 736 | — Madonna del Rosario | " | j |
| 649 | **A. v. d. Neer.** Winter Landscape | Brunswick | j gr |
| 650 | — Winter Landscape | Berlin | i |
| 651 | — Moonshine Landscape | " | i |
| 694 | **E. v. d. Neer.** Woman Playing Guitar | Dresden | r |
| 688 | **Netscher, C.** The Letter Writer | Dresden | i |
| 689 | — The Sick Woman | " | j |
| 690 | — The Music Lesson | " | i |
| 691 | — Shepherd and Shepherdess | Brunswick | j gr |
| 586 | **A. v. Ostade.** Portrait of an Old Woman | Berlin | i |
| 587 | — Studio of the Artist | Dresden | r |
| 588 | — Village Inn | " | i |
| 589 | — Tavern | " | i |
| 590 | — The Annunciation | Brunswick | j gr |
| 591 | **J. v. Ostade.** Winter Amusement | Dresden | r |
| 581 | **Palamedesz.** Portrait of a Young Girl | Berlin | i |
| 582 | — Portrait of a Boy | " | i |
| 271 | **Palma Vecchio.** Female Portrait | " | i   j |
| 272 | — The Three Sisters | Dresden | e   i   j |
| 273 | — Madonna and Child | " | i   j |
| 274 | — Venus | " | e   i   j |
| 46 | **Patinier.** Repose on the Flight into Egypt | Berlin | i |
| 613 | **Bonaventura Peeters.** On the Shore of a Large River | Brunswick | j |
| 207 | **Pencz.** Portrait of a Young Man | Berlin | j |
| 159 | **Pennacchi.** Christ in his Tomb Supported by Angels | " | j |
| 109 | **Perugino.** Madonna, and Child with St. John | London | i |
| 110 | — Archangel St. Michael, Madonna and Child, and Archangel, St. Rafael and Tobias | " | i |
| 111 | — Virgin and Child with Saints and Angels | Paris | r f |
| 823 | **Pesne.** Portrait of the Engraver Schmidt and His Wife | Berlin | i   j |
| 824 | — Portrait of Frederick the Great | " | i   j |

* The letters e n i r f gr indicate the editions published of the respective picture. For prices see p. 76.

| | | | |
|---|---|---|---|
| 825 | **Pesne.** Portrait of Himself | Dresden | i |
| 826 | — Portrait of a Young Lady from Salzburg | Brunswick | f |
| 102 | **Piero di Cosimo.** Venus, Cupid, and Mars | Berlin | f |
| 711 | **Pierson.** Fruitpiece | " | f |
| 113 | **Pinturicchio.** Portrait of a Youth | Dresden | i |
| 246 | **Seb. del Piombo.** Christ Bearing the Cross | " | i f |
| 484 | **Poelemburg.** Landscape with Nymphs and a Dancing Satyr | Brunswick | f |
| 80 | **Pollajuolo.** The Annunciation | Berlin | f |
| 81 | — The Annunciation | Dresden | i |
| 82 | — Wisdom | Florence | f |
| 83 | — St. Sebastian | " | f |
| 84 | — Madonna Adoring the Child | London | i |
| 139 | **Pordenone.** A Woman in Black | Dresden | i |
| 609 | **Potter.** A Herd | " | i |
| 610 | — Cattle | " | i |

67. BOTTICELLI—THE VIRGIN AND CHILD ENTHRONED WITH ANGELS.

| | | | |
|---|---|---|---|
| 339 | **Pourbus the Elder.** Portrait | Dresden | i |
| 340 | — Man with Glass | Brunswick | f gr |
| 801 | **Poussin.** Landscape (The Roman Campagna) | Berlin | i |
| 802 | — Armida Bearing away Rinaldo | " | i |
| 803 | — Infant Jupiter Fed by the Goat Amalthea | " | i |
| 804 | — Time Extracting Truth from Calumny | Paris | f |
| 8010 | — Bacchantic Scene | Cassel | i |
| 629 | **Pynacker, A.** Italian Landscape with Mules | Brunswick | f gr |
| 592 | **Quast, P.** Gin Seller | Brunswick | f gr |
| 216 | **Rafael,** Madonna Colonna | Berlin | e i f |
| 217 | — Madonna with the Gold Finch | " | i f |
| 218 | — Madonna Terranuova | " | i f |
| 219 | — Madonna and Child with St. Jerome and St. Francis | " | f |
| 220 | — Madonna and Child with St. John | " | i f |

* The letters e n i r f gr indicate the editions published of the respective picture. For prices see p. 76.

*In the reproduction of the ancient paintings by the GRAVURE process most extraordinary results have been obtained, notably in our collection of one hundred paintings in the BRUNSWICK GALLERY, and the recent publication of REMBRANDT'S PICTURES IN THE CASSEL GALLERY.*

664.    JACOB RUYSDAEL—WATERFALL.

| | | | | | | |
|---|---|---|---|---|---|---|
| 221 | **Rafael.** Madonna di San Sisto (for particulars see p. 102) | Dresden | e | i | f gr |
| 222 | — Madonna and Child (oval portion of the foregoing) | " | | n i | |
| 222c | — The same (square) | " | e | | |
| 223 | — St. Sixtus | " | e | | |
| 224 | — St. Barbara | " | e | | |
| 225 | — Cherubs | " | | n i | |
| 226 | — La Vierge d'Aldobrandini | London | | | r |
| 227 | — Sta. Catharina of Alexandria | " | | i | |
| 228 | — Vision of a Knight | " | | | f |
| 229 | — La Belle Jardinière | Paris | | i | f |
| 230 | — La Vierge au Voile | " | | i | f |
| 231 | — La Sainte Famille de François I. | " | | | f |
| 232 | — Portrait of Jean d'Arragon | " | | | f |
| 233 | — Portrait of Himself | " | | | r f |
| 234 | — Abundantia (Model of a Fountain) | " | | | f |
| 235 | — Portrait of Himself | Florence | | | f |
| 236 | — Madonna del Granduca | " | | | f |
| 237 | — Cardinal Bibbiena | " | | | f |
| 238 | — Magdalena Doni | Florence | | | f |
| 239 | — Angelo Doni | " | | | f |
| 240 | — La Madonna della Seggiola (called "Sedia") | " | | | f |
| 241 | — Holy Family | " | | | f |
| 242 | — The Vision of Ezechiel | " | | | f |
| 474 | **Ravesteyn.** Portrait of a Man in Armor | Dresden | | i | |
| 475 | — Large Portrait of a Family | Brunswick | | | f gr |
| 501 | **Rembrandt.** Saskia | Berlin | | i | f |
| 502 | — Portrait of Himself | " | | i | f |
| 503 | — Young Woman as Judith | " | | | f |
| 504 | — Joseph's Dream | " | | | f |
| 505 | — The Rape of Proserpina | " | | | f |
| 506 | — Susannah and the Elders | " | | i | f |
| 507 | — The Vision of Daniel | " | | | f |
| 508 | — Landscape (Dutch Low Lands) | " | | | f |
| 509 | — Portrait of Himself | " | | i | |
| 510 | — Ganymede | " | e | i | f |
| 511 | — Portrait of a Man | " | e | i | f |

* *The letters e n i r f gr indicate the editions published of the respective picture. For prices see p. 76.*

| 512 | **Rembrandt.** Saskia | Dresden | | i | f |
| 513 | — Rembrandt and Saskia | " | e | i | f |
| 514 | — Portrait of Himself | " | | i | f |
| 515 | — Portrait of an Old Woman | London | | i | |
| 516 | — Portrait of a Man | " | | i | |
| 517 | — Portrait of Himself | " | | i | |
| 518 | — Portrait of an Unknown Man | Brunswick | | | f gr |
| 519 | — Portrait of the Wife of the Unknown Man | " | | | f gr |
| 520 | — Christ and Magdalen | " | | | f gr |
| 521 | — Landscape with Storm | " | | | f gr |
| 522 | — Portrait of a Family | " | | i | f gr |

*Rembrandt's Etchings.* A collection of 165 Photographs from the choicest etchings in the possession of the Royal Museum, Berlin:

Price, 50 cents (small folio size). A few copies in smaller size at 20 cents each. Price of the entire set, $75.00.
*Rembrandt's paintings in the Gallery of Cassel.* A portfolio containing 17 Gravures on Japan paper. For particulars see Part VI.
*Portrait of Saskia* (from the above portfolio), Gravure Edition de Luxe, printed on Satin, $4.00.

| 759 | **Guido Reni.** Ecce Homo | Dresden | | i | f |
| 760 | — Venus and Cupid | " | e | i | f |
| 761 | — The Annunciation | Paris | | i | f |
| 762 | — The Virgin Mary | " | | i | f |
| 763 | — Cephalus and Procris | Brunswick | | | f gr |
| 863 | **Reynolds.** Portrait of Two Gentlemen | London | | | |
| 719 | **Ribera.** Martyrdom of Bartholomew | Berlin | | | f |
| 720 | — Holy Family | " | e | i | f |
| 721 | — Diogenes | Dresden | | r | |
| 722 | — Sancta Maria of Egypt | " | e | i | f |
| 723 | — Adoration of the Shepherds | Paris | | i | f |
| 724 | — Entombment of Christ | " | | | f |
| 725 | — Portrait of the Painter Zurbaran | Brunswick | | | f |
| 7190 | — Mater Dolorosa | Cassel | | i | |

132.   LIONARDO DA VINCI—MONA LISA.

* The letters e w i r f gr indicate the editions published of the respective picture.   For prices see p. 76.

| | | | | |
|---|---|---|---|---|
| 522 | Rigaud. Portrait of the Dutchess Elizabeth Charlotte of Orleans | Brunswick | | f gr |
| 209 | **Ludger tom Ring the Younger.** The Wedding at Cana | Berlin | i | |
| 251 | **Giulio Romano.** Madonna della Catina | Dresden | e i | |
| 672 | **Rombouts.** Landscape, Woods | Brunswick | | f |
| 326 | **Marinus von Romerswale.** Two Usurers | London | r | |
| 781 | **Salvator Rosa.** Mountain Landscape | Berlin | | f |
| 790 | **Rotari.** St. Magdalen | Dresden | i | f |
| 355 | **Rubens.** The Resurrection of Lazarus | Berlin | e i | f |
| 356 | — Infant Christ with Infant John and Angels | " | e i | f |
| 357 | — Perseus Liberating Captive Andromeda | " | e i | f |
| 358 | — St. Cecilia | " | e i | f |
| 359 | — Neptune and Amphitrite | " | | f |
| 360 | **Rubens and Snyder's** Diana at the Chase | " | n r | f |
| 361 | **Rubens.** Bust of a Man | " | | f |
| 362 | — St. Sebastian | " | | f |
| 363 | — Pieta | " | | f |
| 364 | — Portrait of One of the Artist's Children | | i | |
| 365 | — Madonna and Child with Saints | Berlin | i | |
| 366 | — Old Man | Dresden | i | f |
| 367 | — Bathseba | " | e i | f |
| 368 | — Portrait of Rubens' Second Wife | " | e i | f |
| 369 | — Portrait of an Old Woman | " | i | |
| 370 | — Portrait of a Young Woman | " | i | |
| 371 | — Portrait of a Young Woman in Black with White Collar | " | i | f |
| 372 | — The Last Judgment | " | e i | f |
| 373 | — The Judgment of Paris | Dresden | i | f |
| 374 | — The Garden of Love | " | e i | f |
| 375 | — Drunken Hercules Supported by a Faun and a Bacchant | " | i | |
| 376 | — Diana and Nymphs | " | e i | f |
| 377 | — Diana and Satyrs | " | i | |
| 378 | — Helen Fourment | " | i | f |
| 379 | — Portrait of a Man | " | i | |
| 380 | — Male Portrait | " | i | |
| 381 | — Meleager and Atalante | " | i | f |
| 382 | — Mercury and Argus | " | i | |
| 383 | — Rubens' Sons | " | e i | f |
| 384 | — St. Jerome | " | i | |
| 385 | — Portrait of a Woman | " | i | f |
| 386 | — Chapeau de Paille | London | i | |
| 387 | — Lot's Flight | Paris | i | f |
| 388 | — Madonna Surrounded by Angels | " | | f |
| 389 | — Christ on the Cross | " | i | f |
| 390 | — The Destiny of Maria de Medici and the Triumph of Truth | " | i | f |
| 391 | — Birth of Maria de Medici | " | i | f |
| 392 | — Education of Maria de Medici | " | i | f |
| 393 | — Henry IV. Receiving the Portrait of Maria de Medici | " | i | f |
| 394 | — Marriage of Maria de Medici | " | i | f |
| 395 | — Maria de Medici Landing in Marseilles | " | i | f |
| 396 | — Marriage of Henry IV. and Maria de Medici | " | i | f |
| 397 | — Birth of Louis XIII. in Fontainebleau | " | i | f |
| 398 | — Henry IV. Going to War against Germany | " | i | f |
| 399 | — Journey of Maria de Medici to Pont de Cé | " | i | f |
| 400 | — Changing the Princess on the River Andaye | " | i | f |
| 401 | — Prosperity under the Reign of Mary | " | i | f |
| 402 | — Majority of Louis XIII. | " | i | f |
| 403 | — Flight of the Queen from Blois | " | i | f |
| 404 | — Maria de Medici Meeting Her Son | " | i | f |
| 405 | — Portrait of Maria de Medici | " | r | f |
| 406 | — Portrait of the Baron Henry de Vicq | " | i | f |

*The letters e n i r f gr indicate the editions published of the respective picture. For prices see p. 76.

185.   HANS HOLBEIN THE YOUNGER—PORTRAIT OF
THE MERCHANT GISZE.

| 407 | **Rubens.**  Portrait of a Lady . | Paris | *i* | *f* |
| 408 | —   Portrait of the Marchese Ambrogio Spinola . | Brunswick | | *f gr* |
| 409 | —   Portrait of a Man . | " | | *f gr* |
| 410 | —   Judith with the Head of Holofernes | " | *i* | *f gr* |
| 411 | —   Portrait of the Duke of Buckingham | Florence | | *f* |
| 3550 | —   Jupiter and Kallisto . | Cassel | *i* | |
| 656 | **Jacob Ruysdael.**  Aroused Sea with Coming Storm | Berlin | *i* | *f* |
| 657 | —   Turbulent Sea | " | | *f* |
| 658 | —   View of the Dam Place in Amsterdam . | " | *i* | |
| 659 | —   Harlem Looking from the Beach . | " | | *f* |
| 660 | —   Deep Forest . | " | | *f* |
| 661 | —   The Cloister . | Dresden | *i* | |
| 662 | —   The Hunt . | " | *i* | *f* |
| 663 | —   The Jew Cemetery | " | *i* | |
| 664 | —   Waterfall . | " | *i* | |
| 665 | —   Mountainous Landscape | Brunswick | | *f gr* |
| 666 | —   Waterfall and Castle . | " | | *f gr* |
| 667 | —   Waterfall and Tower . | " | | *f gr* |
| 602 | **Ryckaert, D.**  The Village Fool . | Dresden | *i* | |
| 137 | **Sacchi.**  Christ on the Cross and Saints . | Berlin | *i* | |
| 112 | **Giovanni Santi.**  Madonna and Saints . | " | | *f* |
| 210 | **Andrea del Sarto.**  Abraham's Sacrifice | Dresden | *i* | |
| 211 | —   Portrait of Himself | London | *i* | |
| 212 | —   Charity . | Paris | | *f* |
| 213 | —   Holy Family . | Florence | | *f* |
| 214 | —   Madonna Enthroned and Child with Saints . | Berlin | *i* | |
| 215 | —   Holy Family with Elizabeth and Infant John (School of Andrea) | " | *i* | |
| 772 | **Sassoferrato.**  Virgin Mary Praying . | Dresden | *i* | |
| 773 | —   Madonna and Child . | Paris | | *f* |

* *The letters e n i r f gr indicate the editions published of the respective picture.  For prices see p. 76*

With reference to the photographic editions specified on page 76, according to the different sizes, the FOLIO SIZE is suitable for collections either to be put unmounted in scrap-books, or mounted for portfolios. The larger sizes are generally framed for wall decorations.

156. BELLINI—LEONARDO LOREDANO.

| | | | | |
|---|---|---|---|---|
| 695 | **Schalcken, G.** Boy Angling | Berlin | | f |
| 696 | — Young Man Playing with a False Face | Brunswick | | f gr |
| 352 | **Schaubroek, P.** St. John the Baptist Preaching | " | | f gr |
| 119 | **Schiavone.** Madonna Enthroned and Child | Berlin | | f |
| 320 | **Schidone.** Landscape with the Repose on the Flight Into Egypt | Brunswick | | f |
| 331 | **Scoreel.** Portrait of a Young Woman | Berlin | | f |
| 332 | — Portrait of Cornelisz Aerntz der Van Dussen | " | | f |
| 471 | **Seghers, D.** Flowers | " | | f |
| 537 | **Seibold.** Male Portrait | Dresden | | r |
| 533 | — Female Portrait | " | | r |
| 114 | **Signorelli.** Panels from an Altar (Left Side: Clara, Magdalen, St. Jerome. Right Side: Augustin, St. Cathrine, Anthony of Padua) | Berlin | e i | f |
| 115 | — Pan, God of Nature | " | | f |
| 697 | **van Slingeland.** The Poultry Dealer | Dresden | | r |
| 440 | **Snyders.** Bear Hunt | Berlin | e i | f |
| 441 | — Cock Fight | " | i | f |
| 442 | — A Boar Hunt | Brunswick | | f gr |
| 116 | **Solario.** Portrait of Giovanni Christoforo Longano | London | i | |
| 117 | — Virgin and Child | Paris | | f |
| 118 | — Head of St. John on a Plate | Paris | | f |
| 734 | **Solimena.** Madonna with Saints | Dresden | i | |
| 735 | — Mater Dolorosa | " | i | |
| 553 | **Sorgh, H.** The Workers of the Vintage | Brunswick | | f gr |
| 554 | — The Fish Dealer | Dresden | i | |
| 641 | **Stech.** Burgomaster Stech Out Walking Before the Gates of Danzig | Brunswick | | f |
| 603 | **Jan Steen.** A Merry Crew | Berlin | | f |
| 604 | — The Garden of the Inn | " | i | |
| 605 | — The Expulsion of Hagar | Dresden | i | |
| 606 | — The Marriage Contract | Brunswick | | f gr |

* The letters e n i r f gr indicate the editions published of the respective picture. For prices see f. 76.

# V.—Reproductions from Old Masters.

515 REMBRANDT—PORTRAIT OF AN OLD WOMAN.

*We have photographs from the collections of REMBRANDT'S ETCHINGS and DÜRER'S WOOD-CUTS, of which particulars will be found on page 104.*

\* *The letters e n i v f gr indicate the editions published of the respective picture. For prices see p. 76.*

| | | | | |
|---|---|---|---|---|
| 278 | **Titian.** Portrait of a Daughter of Robert Strozzi . | Berlin | c i f |
| 279 | — Lavinia . | " | c i f |
| 280 | — The Tribute Money | Dresden | u i f |
| 281 | — Girl with Fan | " | i f |
| 282 | — Girl with Vase | " | c i f |
| 283 | — Madonna Di Lucrezia Borgia . | " | c i f |
| 284 | — Madonna and Woman in White | " | c i f |
| 285 | — Part of the Above . | " | c |
| 286 | — Lavinia . | " | i |
| 287 | — Venus Reposing . | " | c i f |
| 288 | — Venus with the Mirror . | " | i f |
| 289 | — A Concert . | London | i |
| 290 | — Madonna and Child with St. John and St. Catherine . | " | i |
| 291 | — Holy Family . | " | i |
| 292 | — Portrait of Francis I | Paris | |
| 293 | — Titian's Mistress . | " | i f |
| 294 | — La Bella di Tiziano | Florence | f |
| 295 | — St. Magdalen . | " | f |
| 296 | — The Redeemer . | " | f |
| 2750 | — Portrait of a Nobleman . | Cassel | i |
| 867 | **Trevisani.** The Triumphal Procession of Galathea | " | i |
| 814 | **de Troy.** Breakfast . | Berlin | f |
| 483 | **Uitewael.** A Feast of the Gods . | Brunswick | f gr |
| 710 | **van Utrecht.** Fruitpiece | " | f |
| 341 | **van Valckenborgh, H.** Rocky Landscape with Mill . | " | |
| 738 | **de Valdes Leal.** St. Basco . | Dresden | i |
| 770 | **Varotari.** Judith . | " | i f |
| 771 | — Study Head . | " | |
| 256 | **Vasari.** Portrait of Cosmo I. of Medici | Berlin | i c f |
| | **Otto van Veen.** See Heemskerk . | | |
| 739 | **Velasquez.** Allessandro del Borro . | " | i f |
| 740 | — Maria Anna, Wife of Ferdinand III | " | i f |
| 741 | — Portrait of a Young Man . | " | i f |
| 742 | — Bust of a Young Man . | Dresden | i f |
| 743 | — Caspar de Guzmann . | Dresden | i f |
| 744 | — Male Portrait . | " | i f |

$32. MME. LE BRUN—PAINTED BY HERSELF.

* The letters c w s r f gr indicate the editions published of the respective picture. For prices see p. 76.

A REDUCTION

OF PRICE,

*subject to a special agreement, will be*

*allowed to purchasers of*

ENTIRE SETS

*of the single schools of art or galleries.*

865. GAINSBOROUGH—PORTRAIT
OF SIR BATE DUDLEY.

\* *The letters c u i r f gr indicate the editions published of the respective picture. For prices see p. 76.*

| | | | |
|---|---|---|---|
| 708 | **Weenix, Jan.** Dead Game | Dresden | i |
| 709 | — Dead Hare and Bird | Berlin | i |
| 855 | **Weitsch.** The Former Oak Forest at Querum, near Brunswick | Brunswick | f |
| 701 | **van der Werff.** Penitent Magdalen | Berlin | f |
| 702 | — Portrait of the Artist and his Family | Dresden | i f |
| 703 | — The Expulsion of Hagar | " | i f |
| 704 | — Penitent Magdalen | " | i f |
| 705 | — Adam and Eve | Brunswick | f gr |
| 706 | — Two Chess Players | " | |
| 27 | **Roger van der Weyden.** Altar of the Chancellor Bladelin (3 pieces) | Berlin | i f |
| 28 | — Altar of St. John (3 panels) | " | i f |
| 29 | — Altar of Miraflores (3 panels) | " | i f |
| 30 | — Descent from the Cross (copy) | " | i |
| 31 | — Christ Crucified | Dresden | f |
| 32 | — Burial of Christ | London | i |

433. VAN DYCK—PORTRAIT OF HIMSELF.

CATALOGUES of Foreign Galleries and Art Exhibitions will cheerfully be procured by us. We shall also gladly give information about foreign publications, and import them if so desired.

| | | | |
|---|---|---|---|
| 33 | **Roger van der Weyden the Younger.** Mater Dolorosa | London | r |
| 34 | — Ecce Homo | " | r |
| 35 | — Portrait of Himself | " | r |
| 36 | — Portrait of His Wife | " | r |
| 489 | **Willaerts, A.** Coast with Church Steeple | Brunswick | f gr |
| 699 | **van der Wilt.** Playing Checkers | Berlin | i f |
| 634 | **Wouvermann, Ph.** Riding School | " | i f |
| 635 | — Rest of a Hunting Party at a River | " | f |
| 636 | — Horses in Front of a Blacksmith's Shop | " | f |
| 637 | — Hay Wagon | " | f |
| 638 | — Starting for a Hunt | Dresden | i f |
| 639 | — Leaving for a Falcon Hunt | " | i f |
| 640 | — Christ Ascending into Heaven | Brunswick | f gr |
| 6340 | — The Return from the Falcon Hunt | Cassel | i |

* The letters e n i r f gr indicate the editions published of the respective picture. For prices see p. 76.

*The letters e n i r f gr indicate the editions published of the respective picture.  For prices see p. 76.*

62.   Filippo Lippi—Madonna Adoring the Child.

# TWO STANDARD WORKS OF

## Rafael.

# "SISTINE MADONNA."

### THE FIRST GRAVURE FROM THIS MASTERWORK.

Size of Plate, 26 × 35 inches.

## PRICE, $15.00.

The important improvements of the photographic process in the last few years have made the issuing of new editions of the most prominent paintings of the European Galleries very desirable.

At the head of the list of such works, as we are about to publish, and to which the portfolio of Rembrandt's pictures of the Cassel Gallery (see Part VI.) is another addition, we have put *Rafael's* "SISTINE MADONNA," and are glad to state, that both our recent photographs and the large gravure, have met with the general approval of all connoisseurs and art critics.

# ANCIENT RELIGIOUS ART.

## Holbein.

# "MADONNA."

### THE FIRST GRAVURE FROM THE ORIGINAL IN DARMSTADT.

Size of Plate, 24½ × 35 inches.

### PRICE, $15.00.

The unforeseen success, which our new edition of the "SISTINE MADONNA" has found, has induced us to apply the same care to the artistic reproduction of another masterpiece, the *Holbein* "MADONNA," which is justly considered the standard work of ancient German religious art.

Our reproduction is taken from the original in the possession of the Grand-duke of Hessen Darmstadt, which was originally painted for the *Burgomaster Meier* of Basel.

# REMBRANDT'S ETCHINGS.

Our collection of photographs from the choicest etchings of this eminent master contains 165 subjects which are in the possession of the Royal Museum, Berlin. The price for each copy (about small folio size) is 50 cents. There is a number of still smaller subjects in this collection which cost only 20 cents each.

We shall be happy to forward, to those who are desirous of acquiring the complete collection, a sample book for reference containing an arrangement of the whole collection.

The demand for these superior specimens of the great Dutch master, increasing year by year, enables us to offer the complete collection for $75.

# ALBRECHT DÜRER.

Photographs from Engravings and Woodcuts of Dürer in the Royal Museum at Berlin.

## SUNDRY SUBJECTS.

34 Subjects in Folio à 70 cts.
12   "     in Cabinet Size à 35 cts.

## 4 SUBJECTS FROM THE REVELATIONS ST. JOHN.

In Folio Size à 70 cts.

## 16 SUBJECTS FROM THE SMALL PASSION.

*From Dürer's Engravings.*

In Cabinet Size à 35 cts.

## LIFE OF THE VIRGIN MARY.

*From Dürer's Original-woodcuts.*

20 Subjects.

In Folio à 70 cts. ; in Cabinet à 35 cts.

## THE LARGE PASSION.

*From Dürer's Original-woodcuts.*

12 Subjects.

In Folio à 70 cts. ; in Cabinet à 35 cts.

## THE SMALL PASSION.

*From Dürer's Original-woodcuts.*

36 Subjects.

In Cabinet Size à 35 cts.

# VI.

## MISCELLANEOUS:

ART PORTFOLIOS, ETC., SCULPTURES AND VIEWS.

SASKIA VAN ULENBURGH.

# Rembrandt

A PORTFOLIO WITH

## 17 PHOTOGRAVURES

DIRECTLY AFTER

## REMBRANDT'S

## ORIGINAL

## PAINTINGS

IN THE

## CASSEL GALLERY.

13 plates measuring about 17½ x 15½ inches each
4    "        "    "    6 x 4½    "    "
all printed on Japan paper.    Price, $75.00.

## TABLE OF CONTENTS

Every connoisseur is aware that among all galleries the one at Cassel can boast of an almost unequalled collection of Rembrandts. Numerically it is the largest but one collection, and in regard to artistic eminence these specimens of Rembrandt's Works rank second to none.

While it goes without saying that no public or private gallery should be without our Rembrandt Work, we appeal, when issuing it, not only to students and the untold number of admirers of the great Dutch master, but to every cultured home, to which we trust it will find its way.

# SECESSION.

A PORTFOLIO OF 62 GRAVURES, FROM PAINTINGS AND
STUDIES BY MEMBERS OF THE " VEREIN BILDEN-
DER KÜNSTLER MÜNCHENS."

*Containing characteristic works by KLINGER,
KUEHL, LIEBERMANN, SKARBI-
NA, STUCK, THOMA, v. UHDE, etc.*

PUBLISHED IN TWO DIFFERENT EDITIONS :

### ARTIST PROOFS ON JAPAN PAPER.
**Each Proof signed by the Artist.**      **Price, $100.**

PRINT EDITION ON INDIA PAPER.
Price, $35.00.

FRONTISPIECE OF THE PORTFOLIO " SECES-
SION," DESIGNED BY MAX KLINGER.

*Referring to this work the New York Tribune, March 25th, 1894, says :*

We have received from the Berlin Photographic Company some plates of an extremely
interesting publication, a portfolio issued in illustration of the work of the Munich "Secessionists." These painters are the men who revolted against the rule of the Academic con-
tingent and gave their art free swing under liberal conditions of their own devising. They
count among their ranks some of the most advanced artists in the German school. Lenbach is
not of the group, but Uhde is, and Max Liebermann, Franz Stuck, Hans Thoma, L. von
Hofmann, Theodor Heine, and Franz Skarbina—in other words, the whole emancipated wing
of German art—have come into the fold. The portfolio referred to is composed of sixty-two
plates done by photographic process and printed well on Japanese paper. *The reproductive
work has been accomplished most satisfactorily,* and the plates give a good idea of an important
movement. They present the individualities of the painters, and, as many of the latter have
entered upon the path of realism plus mysticism, which has been in vogue recently in Paris
and London, the interesting nature of the publication may be imagined. The " Adam and
Eve " of Franz Stuck, now before us, is a remarkable composition. The attention of amateurs
is directed toward what is without question a valuable side-light on one phase of modern European art.

*The Collector, published by A. Trumble, writes :*

The Berlin Photographic Company has made an admirable album of photogravures from
pictures by the clique of Munich artists who have taken as a title for themselves that of the
Secessionists. Artistic Munich keeps a close eye on Paris, and when something occurs on the
banks of the Seine, something kindred in Nature occurs on the banks of the Isar, afterwards.
The secession movement probably had its inception in the upheaval in Paris which created
the new Salon. As they could not get a footing in Munich, the Secessionists went to Berlin,
where they made their first show, and as they included in their ranks men of such merit as
Max Liebermann, Fritz von Uhde, Skarbina, Klinger, and Kuehl, it was but natural that
their display should make a hit. Following up their Berlin success, the Society established
itself on its own account in Munich, but its Berlin commencement had made a mark, which
that city, always in rivalry with Munich as an art centre, was not slow to take advantage of.
The result of this rivalry, always amiable but always active, was the production by the Berlin
Photographic Company of the album of some sixty odd plates from their productions. *The
reproductions in the " Album " are deliciously beautiful and it is a work which deserves a place
in every art-lover's collection.*

## MAX LIEBERMANN'S ETCHINGS.

A PORTFOLIO OF ORIGINAL ETCHINGS WITH TEXT BY DR. RICHARD GRAUL.

Only 100 copies published.     Price, $35.00.

# The Brunswick Gallery,

EDITED BY DIRECTOR HERMANN RIEGEL.

## 100 *PHOTOGRAVURES FROM THE ORIGINALS,*

*Folio Size, about 7 x 9 inches.*

| | |
|---|---:|
| *In embossed leather binding* | . $150.00 |
| *In calico portfolio* | . 100.00 |

## Peter von Cornelius.

### CARTOONS OF THE FRESCOES OF THE GLYPTOTHEK IN MUNICH.

From the originals in the National Gallery at Berlin.

| | |
|---|---:|
| *Published in extra size*, 14 *numbers complete* . . . . . . | . $100.00 |
| 14 *folio photographs in portfolio* . . . . . . . | . $10.00 |
| *Single numbers in extra size*, $15 *each ; in imperial*, $4 *each : folio size* $1.00 *each*. | |

### CARTOONS OF THE HOHENZOLLERN TOMB (CAMPO SANTO).

From the originals in the National Gallery at Berlin.

*Published in extra size*, 17 *numbers complete in portfolio*, $150 ; *single numbers* . $12.00 *each*
*Published in folio size*, 9 *numbers in tasteful portfolio*, $10 ; *single numbers* $1.00 *each*.

## Posthumous Works by Alfred Rethel.

Photographs from original drawings.

| | |
|---|---:|
| 32 *numbers in imperial size* @ . | $2.50 *each* |
| 50 *numbers in folio size* @ . | $1.00 *each* |

## PORTFOLIOS. *With Selected Photographs from the best works of art of the following Galleries :*

### Berlin Gallery—Dresden Gallery—The National Gallery at Berlin.

*Each portfolio containing* 15 *photographs in folio size* @ . . $10.00

# Artist=Albums.

CONTAINING A SELECTION OF THE MOST PROMINENT WORKS OF THE RESPECTIVE MASTERS.

Each album contains 15 photographs in folio size (size of mount 12 x 15 inches), in calico portfolio, gold-embossed cover.   Full contents of each album will be furnished on application.
Price of each album . . . . . . . . . . . . . . . . . . $10.00

W. Amberg=Album.
Carl Becker=Album.
Hans Dahl=Album.
Ed. Gruetzner=Album.
Ludwig Knaus=Album.

Meyer von Bremen=Album.
Gustav Richter=Album
(21 photographs in folio size, in leather
portfolio, $12.)
B. Vautier=Album.

---

**Falat, Julius.** SOUVENIR OF THE BEAR HUNT OF KAISER WILHELM II. IN
NIESWIEZ, 1886.  10 photographs from water-color paintings in canvas portfolio . $12.00

**Gruetzner, Ed.** FALSTAFF SERIES.  7 folio photographs in calico portfolio, with German
text by Prof. Dr. Heigel in Munich.  Price  . . . . . . . . . $7.50

**Richter, Gustav.** PORTRAIT ALBUM, containing 20 photographs in portfolio  . $15.00

**Schirmer, J. W.** LANDSCAPES FROM THE BIBLE.
6 pair of photographs in imperial size, with portfolio . . . $20.00
Edition in folio size . . . . . . . $7.50

**v. Werner, Anton, and Bracht, E.** PANORAMA OF THE BATTLE OF SEDAN.
8 folio photographs in portfolio . . . . . . . $7.50

**The Franco=German War, 1870=71.**  15 photographs from original paintings by Adam
Bleibtreu, Camphausen, Freiberg, Hünten, von Werner.
Folio size, in calico portfolio, price  . . . . . $10.00

**Sporting Scenes.**  15 photographs from original paintings, by Camphausen, von Ernst,
Freiberg, Koch, Steffeck.
Folio size in calico portfolio  . $10.00

**Hunting Scenes.**  15 photographs from original paintings, by Deiker, Freese, Henke, Kröner,
Sperling, Steffeck.
Folio size, in calico portfolio . $10.00

**Pfannschmidt, C. G.** WECKSTIMMEN AUS DER HEILIGEN SCHRIFT.
Eight compositions from Scripture.
Edition in photogravures, with artistic binding . . $5.00
Edition in heliogravures, elegantly bound . . $6.00

**Raffael's** AMOR AND PSYCHE.  (From the frescoes in Villa Farnesina in Rome).
With German text by C. F. Waagen.  Folio edition, 12 numbers, in calico portfolio . $10.00

"Bildernovellen," }
"Künstlerhumor." }  Two fine Art Books with photogravures, text in German.
Price of each book in gilt and edges . . . . . $7.50

# SCULPTURES.

### PHOTOGRAPHS FROM ORIGINAL ANCIENT WORKS OF SCULPTURE AND OF CASTS
in the Royal Museum at Berlin.

### FOLIO SIZE, UNMOUNTED, .    . 75c.

## MODERN WORKS OF SCULPTURE

Photographed from the originals in the National Gallery at Berlin.

Special Catalogue mailed on application.

# VIEWS
## OF BERLIN, POTSDAM, AND VICINITY,

Taken from nature.

FOLIO SIZE, UNMOUNTED, .    .    .    .    .    50c.

List of views mailed on application.

THE BRANDENBURG GATE IN BERLIN.

# 1895

## SUPPLEMENT

### TO THE

# CATALOGUE

#### OF THE

## BERLIN PHOTOGRAPHIC COMPANY

### FINE ART PUBLISHERS

## 14 EAST TWENTY-THIRD STREET

### MADISON SQUARE (SOUTH)

## NEW YORK

NOTICE : The present supplement contains all our new publications since the issue of our Illustrated Catalogue of 1894 up to October 1, 1895. The edition published thereof and prices will be found in each respective part, with the exception of the photographs mentioned in Part III., of which the following table gives an explanation regarding sizes and prices.

## PHOTOGRAPHS

Most of the photographs are published in different sizes, indicated by the letters *e, n, i, r, f,* after each title, as follows.

| | | | | |
|---|---|---|---|---|
| *e* = Extra, size of mount 35½x47 inches | | | Price, $15 00 |
| *n* = Normal, size " 31½x43 " | | | " 10 00 |
| *i* = Imperial, size " 26 x33½ " | | | " 4 00 |
| *r* = Royal, size " 19½x25½ " . . . . . . | | | " 3 00 |
| *f* = Folio, size either mounted as *Boudoir Cards on black cardboard*, size about 8x10 inches . . | | | " 1 00 |
| Or as *Folio on India Paper* 15x20 inches | | | " 1 00 |

III

# I.

# ARTISTS' PROOFS

## L. Alma=Tadema

SPRING (Size 35x15½ inches.)

    250 *Japan Proofs*                                              *all sold*

    150 *India Proofs*                                             *all sold*

Copyright 1895 by Photographische Gesellschaft.

*Between the marble columns of a narrow street winds one of those processions which have so frequently taken place on religious festivals at Athens and Rome. In the foreground of the picture a few steps lead down to the level of the pavement, crowded with the joyful procession. Bare-footed children carrying baskets out of which they strew the fragrant blossoms of the welcome Spring-time, lead the way, accompanied by a few maidens who bear further witnesses of the awakening Spring in their hands. They are followed by servants of the Temple of Flora, playing on lyres and cymbals, and carrying the statuettes of Pan, the great symbol of Nature. We observe the reverend face of the priest behind this group under the shade of a banner carried by two slaves, followed by virgins with palms in their hands. An innumerable mass of followers is seen far back into the distant street.*

*The rapture of this procession seems to find a hundred-fold echo in the mass of spectators who watch the procession from the balustrades, windows, and balconies of the houses, whose marble columns are wound with garlands, and from whose very tops arises incense to greet the Goddess of Spring.*

(For Prints see p. 117.)

FORTUNE'S FAVORITE (Size 17½x12½ inches.)

    400 *Japan Proofs* . . . . . . $20 00

W. DENDY SADLER, "A CURE FOR GOUT."

Copyright 1893 by Photographische Gesellschaft.

## S. Anderson

A FLIGHT OF DOVES (Size 11½x20 inches.)

    100 *India Proofs*                               $15 00

## Th. Blinks

A COUPLE FROM THE OAKLEY (Size 14½x19½ inches.)

    50 *India Proofs*                               15 00

HARK TO FOWLER (Size 14½x22 inches.)

    150 *India Proofs*                              20 00

NOW RIDE, LADS! (Size 15x22 inches.)

    150 *India Proofs*                              20 00

## M. Dicksee

THE FIRST AUDIENCE (Oliver Goldsmith reading his Vicar of Wakefield,)  (Size 14x20½ inches.)

    50 *India Proofs*                               15 00

## A. J. Elsley

WAIT A MINUTE (Size 20½x15 inches.)

    150 *India Proofs*                              15 00

## L. Falero

TOWARDS A BETTER WORLD (Size 20½x12½ inches.)

    150 *India Proofs*                              15 00

## J. Farquharson

OVER SNOWFIELDS WASTE AND PATHLESS (Size 22½x17½ inches.)

150 *India Proofs*                                                    $20 00

L. FALERO,
" TOWARD A BETTER WORLD."

## J. W. Godward

YES OR NO? (Size 30x16 inches.)

*India Proofs*          .                                *all sold*

## Maude Goodman

SUSPENSE (Size 16½x29 inches.)

200 *India Proofs* .                                         25 00

## Heywood Hardy

A GIRL OF THE PERIOD.

25 *India Proofs* .                                         15 00

## Talbot Hughes

THE STIRRUP CUP (Size 9½x7½ inches.)

200 *India Proofs* .     .                                 10 00

Copyright 1895 by Photographische
Gesellschaft.

## B. W. Leader

SOLITUDE (Size 22x17½ inches.)

50 *Japan Proofs*                                          30 00
150 *India Proofs*                                         20 00

## E. Blair Leighton

JUST BY CHANCE (Size 11½x8 inches.)

200 *Japan Proofs*                                         15 00
200 *India Proofs*                                         10 00

## Sir Fr. Leighton

ATALANTA (Size 12½x8 inches.)

*India Proofs*          .                                *all sold*

PHOEBE (Size 16½x14½ inches.)

200 *Japan Proofs*                                         20 00
200 *India Proofs*                                         15 00

## John A. Lomax

TO BRING THE ROSES BACK (Size 13½x20 inches.)
    50 *India Proofs*         .         $15 00

## Briton Rivière

THE EMPTY CHAIR (Size 14x20 inches.)
    100 *India Proofs*   .       .   -     .     15 00

## H. Ryland

NEAERA (Size 13½x9 inches.)
    150 *India Proofs*         15 00

## W. Dendy Sadler

A CURE FOR GOUT (Size 13x19 inches.)
    200 *Japan Proofs*   .    .   .   .     20 00
    200 *India Proofs*   .    .   .   .     15 00

## A. Sawyer

EVOE ! IO BACCHE ! (Size 7½x22½ inches.)
    20 *India Proofs on etching paper*     15 00

## J. M. Strudwick

GOLDEN STRINGS (Size 14½x10 inches.)
    75 *Japan Proofs*       .     20 00
    75 *India Proofs*       .     15 00

## A. W. Strutt

LIVE AND LET LIVE (Size 14½x20 inches.)
    40 *India Proofs*   .   .     15 00

## F. v. Uhde

ENTOMBMENT OF CHRIST (Size 21x29 inches.)
    100 *Japan Proofs*   .   .   .     30 00

E. BLAIR LEIGHTON,
"JUST BY CHANCE."

Copyright 1895 by Photographische
Gesellschaft.

## II.

## FACSIMILE GRAVURES IN COLORS.

| | | |
|---|---|---:|
| **Ballavoine, J.** L'envolée (Une charmeuse.) 10 × 7 inches. | ⎱ Companions. each | |
| — Les papillons séduits. 10 × 7 inches. | ⎰ | $6.00 |
| **Bedini, P.** Malheur, si la pelotte tombe ! (The lost thread.) 10 × 14 inches. | ⎱ Companions. each | |
| — Souvenir d'un voyage de nôce. 10 × 14 inches. | ⎰ | 10.00 |
| **Dietrich, A.** Christ's sermon on the mount. 21 × 11 inches. | | 13.50 |
| **Eismann–Semenowski.** Pierrette. 10½ × 7 inches. | | 6.00 |
| **Perez, A.** Pour rien au monde. 7 × 5½ inches. | ⎱ Companions. each | |
| — Madame est sortie. 7 × 5½ inches. | ⎰ | 5.00 |

EISMANN-SEMENOWSKI, " PIERRETTE."

Copyright 1895 by Photographische Gesellschaft.

# III.

# PHOTOGRAPHS AND GRAVURE PRINTS

ARRANGED

## ALPHABETICALLY ACCORDING TO THE NAMES OF THE ARTISTS.

| No. | ARTIST AND TITLE. | Photographs. | Gravure Prints. |
|---|---|---|---|
| 2492 | **Achenbach.** A Mill in Moonlight | | 13½x20½ 85 |
| 2429 | **Alma Tadema L.** Spring (for Artist's Proofs see p. 112.) | | 35½x16 16 50 |
| 2520 | — Fortune's Favorite (for Artist's Proofs see p. 112.) | | |
| 2515 | **Anderson, S.** A Flight of Doves (for Artist's Proofs see p. 113.) | | |
| 2442 | **Assmus, R.** Reveille before the Castle of Hohenzollern | i   f | |
| 2473 | **Ballavoine, J.** L'envolée (for facsimile Gravures see p. 116.) | | |
| 2474 | — Les papillons séduits (for facsimile Gravures see p. 116) | | |
| 2511 | **Barlösius, G.** Queen Luise with the Princes on her journey to Tilsit | f | |
| 2525 | **Barstow, M.** A Prude on the Prowl | f | |
| 2441 | **Barthel, P.** Revery | f | |
| 2426 | **Beckert, P.** Sacred Heart | | |
| 2451 | **Bedini, P.** The Lost Thread (see facsimilie gravures p. 116) | | |
| 2452 | — Reminiscences of a Honeymoon (see facsimile gravures, p. 116) | | |
| 2465 | **Bisson, E.** Au bal | r   f | |
| 2466 | — En observation | r   f | |
| 2467 | — L'amour entraînant la jeunesse | r   f | |

\* The letters e n i r f indicate the sizes in which the photos are published. For prices see p. 111.

| | ARTIST AND TITLE. | Photographs ... | Gravures. Size. Price. |
|---|---|---|---|
| 2470 | **Blinks, Th.** A Couple from the Oakley (for Artist's Proofs see p. 113) | | |
| 2482 | — Hark to Fowler } (for Artist's Proofs see p. | | |
| 2483 | — Now Ride, Lads } 113) | | |
| 2469 | **Block, J.** An Accord | | 10x15½ $3 |
| 2500 | **Bodenhausen, C. v.** An Autumn Song | i f | |
| 2423 | **Briton Rivière.** The Empty Chair (for Artist's Proofs see p. 115) | | 14x20½ 5 |
| 2414 | **Clementz, H.** The Great Elector Receiving the African Chief Janke | n i f | |
| 2460 | **Corelli, A.** The Mother | | 12½x22½ 6 |
| 2439 | **Dietrich, A.** Sermon on the Mountain (see facsimile Gravures p. 116) | n i f | 21x11 5 |
| 2453 | — Lord, Take Pity on Us | i f | 15x21 5 |
| 2504 | **Eismann-Semenowski.** Pierrette (for facsimile Gravures see p. 116) | | |
| 2434 | **Elsley, A. J.** Wait a Minute (for Artist's Proofs see p. 113) | f | 21x15 5 |
| 2413 | **Falero.** Towards a Better World (for Artist's Proofs see p. 113.) | f | 21x12½ 5 |
| 2433 | **Farguharson, J.** Over Snowfields, Waste and Pathless (for Artist's Proofs see p. 114) | | 23x17⅞ 7 50 |
| 2481 | **Fellowes, Prynne.** Magnificat (Madonna and Child Surrounded by Angels) | i f | |
| 2448 | **Firle, W.** Give us this Day Our Daily Bread | f | |
| 2449 | — Thy Will Be Done | f | |
| 2450 | — Forgive Us Our Trespasses | f | |
| 2427 | **Gallegos, J.** Holy Communion | r f | |
| 2519 | — The Mass | r f | |
| 2454 | **Gebhardt, E. v.** I Will Not Let Thee, Except Thee Bless Me | | 18x12 5 |
| 2497 | **Goodman, Maude.** Suspense (for Artist's Proofs see p. 114) | | |
| 2490 | **Hardy, Heywood.** A Likely Draw | | 20½x13½ 5 |
| 2491 | — A Girl of the Period (for Artist's Proofs see p. 114) | f | |
| 2422 | **Hitchens, A.** Legend of the Christmas Rose | f | |
| 2443 | **Hoffman, H.** Head of Christ | f | |
| 2498 | **Hughes, Talbot.** The Stirrup Cup (for Artist's Proofs see p. 114.) | | |
| 2440 | **Kehren, J.** Madonna | i f | |
| 2517 | **Koch, H.** Judgment of Paris | n i f | |
| 2431 | **Koner, M.** Emperor William II. | i f | |
| 2420 | **Kröner, Chr.** Woodcocks | r f | |
| 2421 | — Mountain Cocks | r f | |
| 2486 | — Pheasants | r | |
| 2487 | — Partridges | r | |
| 2503 | **Laudini, A.** Fleurette | f | |
| 2510 | — La bienvenue de la jeune épouse | i f | |
| 2425 | **Leader, B. W.** Solitude (for Artist's Proofs see p. 114) | | 22x17½ 7 50 |
| 2476 | **Leighton, E. Blair.** Just by Chance (for Artist's Proofs see p. 114) | | 11½x 8 3 |
| 2475 | **Leighton, Sir Frederick.** Phoebe (for Artist's Proofs see p. 114) | | |
| 2477 | **Lenbach, F. v.** Portrait of Bismarck painted in 1894. 50 prints on Japan paper at $15.00 | | 28½x24 12 |
| 2410 | **Lieck, J.** Prayer of Thanks | i f | |
| 2501 | — Carina | r f | |
| 2485 | **Lomax, John A.** To Bring the Roses Back (for Artist's Proofs see p. 116). | f | 13½x20 5 |
| 2522 | **Lossow, H.** Old Roman | r f | |

* The letters e n i r f indicate the sizes in which the photos are published. For prices see p. 111.

| No. | ARTIST AND TITLE | Photograph Sizes* | Gravure Size | Price |
|---|---|---|---|---|
| 2463 | Madrazo, R.  La belle anglaise | f | | |
| 2493 | March, T.  Un baptème en Espagne | | 14x20½ | $5 |
| 2489 | Max-Ehrler L.  An Order for Santa-Claus | f | | |
| 2479 | Menzler, W.  In Maiden Meditation, Fancy Free | i  f | | |
| 2437 | Müller, C.  Madonna (oval, part from No. 733) | i  r  f | | |
| 2447 | — Madonna (round, part from No. 1589) | i | | |
| 2416 | Müller, Frz.  Marriage of St. Mary and St. Joseph | i  f | | |
| 2417 | — The Holy Family at Work | i  f | | |
| 2418 | — Christ in the Temple | i  f | | |
| 2419 | — Death of St. Joseph | i  f | | |
| 2464 | Munier, E.  The Child's Prayer | i  f | | |
| 2473 | Munthe, L.  Evening in the Forest (Winter scene) | | 12x21 | 5 |
| 2438 | Naujok, G.  St. Cecilia (Bust) | i  f | | |
| 2396 | Nonnenbruch, M.  Christian Woman Praying | | 20¼x12 | 5 |
| 2518 | — Iphigenia | f | | |
| 2526 | Orczy, E.  Devouring the News | f | | |
| 2499 | Papperitz, G.  Diana at the Hunt | n  i  f | | |
| 2524 | Parker, Sybil C.  The Door of the Fold | i  f | | |
| 2387 | Pauwels, Fr.  "If Thou Seek Him with all Thy Heart, etc." | | 13⅞x21 | 5 |
| 2455 | Perez, A.  Tit for Tat | i  f | | |
| 2456 | — Public bal | i  f | | |
| 2457 | — Pour rien au monde (see facsimile gravures p. 116) | | | |
| 2458 | — Madame est sortie (see facsimile gravures p. 116) | | | |
| 2506 | Perrault, L.  Bonne petite mère | i  f | | |
| 2033 | Pötzelberger, R.  Harmony | r | | |
| 2428 | Raupp, K.  Evening | f | | |
| 2415 | Richter, O. D. v.  Lucas Cranach Asking Catherine Bora's Hand for Dr. Martin Luther | i  f | | |
| 2462 | Roeber, Fr.  The Last State Council of the Great Elector | n  i  f | | |
| 2411 | Rödig, M.  Mozart | i  f | 20x16 | 5 |
| 2412 | — Mozart (Bust) | i  f | 17½x13½ | 5 |
| 2351 | — Beethoven | | 20x16 | 5 |
| 2352 | — Beethoven (Bust) | | 17½x13½ | 5 |
| 2513 | — Schiller | i  f | | |
| 2514 | — Goethe | i  f | | |
| 2444 | Roessler, A. v.  Lieutenant v. Schmeling at Ligny | i  f | | |
| 2508 | — Durch! | r | | |
| 2450 | Royer, L.  Notre Dame de Lourdes | i  f | | |
| 2505 | — The Triumph of Venus | i  f | 21x10½ | 5 |
| 2446 | Ryland, H.  Neaera (for Artist's Proofs see p. 115) | | 13½x9 | 3 |
| 2484 | Sadler W. Dendy.  A Cure for Gout (for Artist's Proofs see p. 115) | | | |
| 2445 | Saltini, P.  The Caricature | i  f | • | |
| 2472 | Sawyer, A.  Evoe! Io Bacche (for Artist's Proofs see p. 115) | | | |
| 2495 | Schmidt, M.  Forestscene | | 14x19½ | 5 |
| 2496 | — Marine | | 14x20 | 5 |
| 2527 | Schmid, J.  Charity | i  f | | |
| 2502 | Seifert, A.  The Echo | i  f | | |
| 2436 | Shields, Fr.  The Annunciation | f | | |
| 2503 | Sichel, N.  Rest on me your dark eyes | i  f | | |
| 2523 | — Sappho | i  f | | |
| 2432 | Sperling, H.  A Tête à Tête | f | | |
| 2516 | Strudwick, J. M.  Golden Strings (for Artist's Proofs see p. 115) | | | |
| 2488 | Strutt, A. W.  Live and let Live (for Artist's Proofs see p. 115) | f | | |
| 2512 | Thoma, H.  Solitude | | | |
| 2424 | Uhde, Fr. v.  Holy Eve | | 16x20 | 5 |
| 2471 | — The Entombment of Christ (for Artist's Proofs see p. 115) | | 21x29 | 12 |

* The letters c n i r f indicate the sizes in which the photos are published.  For prices see p. 111.

| No. | ARTIST AND TITLE. | Photographic Sizes.* | | Sizes. | Gravures. Price. |
|---|---|---|---|---|---|
| 2430 | **Veith, E.**  Madonna . | i | f | 13½x19 | $5 |
| 2507 | **Wagner, C.**  Beethoven | i | f | | |
| 2461 | **Weisz, A.**  Othello and Desdemona . | i | f | 13½x20½ | 5 |
| 1671 | **Werner, A. v.**  Proclamation of the German Emperor at Versailles, 1871 . | | | 16x19 | 5 |
| 2521 | **Wierusz Kowalski, A.**  Winternight in Litthauen | | | | |
| 2463 | **Wünnenberg, C.**  On the Banks of the Peneios . | i | f | | |

*The letters e n i r f indicate the sizes in which the photos are published. For prices see p. 111.

JOHN A. LOMAX, "TO BRING THE ROSES BACK."